THE LEGEND OF THE SEA

The Spectacular Marine Photography of Gilles Martin-Raget

THE LEGEND OF THE SEA

The Spectacular Marine Photography of
Gilles Martin-Raget

Contents

p. 4–5
A small boat on a turquoise sea. The pure delights of sailing in the sheltered waters of the Santa-Manza Gulf in south Corsica.

p. 6–7
Moonbeam of Fife III has her work cut out against the Mediterranean waves, much to the delight of the Voiles de Saint-Tropez crew and the spectators at the shore.

p. 8–9
A final bearing away towards victory for the *Oracle Team USA* against *Team New Zealand*, during the last and decisive race of the spectacular America's Cup, which took place in San Francisco in September 2013.

Opposite page
A nice breeze and a close crossing between the tall ships *Amerigo Vespucci*, *Alexander von Humboldt II* and *Mir* off the Toulon coast in September 2013.

INTRODUCTION

One hand for the man, one hand for the photo

Sometimes photography represents an unwarranted onslaught on the senses, as it did through the roads of the slightly sleepy old town of Arles on the River Rhône, between the regions of Camargue and Provence, where I was fortunate enough to be born and where I grew up. It may have happened on a warm summer's evening, which I spent in the courtyard of the archbishop's palace, staring wide-eyed at the projections of Les Recontres Arles Photographie (the annual international photographic exhibition).

Maybe the bug took hold more deeply on the beaches of the Camargue, where sky and wind truly show what they can be capable of, sculpting the driftwood brought ashore by the sea breeze. It was an ideal backdrop for me to experiment, using my first camera given to me as a birthday present. This was inevitably followed by more or less controlled chemical sessions messing around with film, which I had poorly fixed in the family bathroom. Too late, the damage was done …

The second phase, this time brought about by professional photography and specifically directed at a maritime subject, hit a few years later in the sea off Newport, Rhode Island, during the 25th America's Cup in 1983. It was a time when the 12-Metres still paraded their elegant silhouettes through the fog around the Brenton Reef Light. The property of American sailors for the previous 132 years, the America's Cup was the exclusive preserve of an army of the very tall and physically strong, who were inaccessible, very sure of themselves, extremely well funded and even better organised. But it was in 1983 that the great upheaval took place, with the sensational victory of the 12-Metre racing yacht *Australia II*, and her revolutionary winged keel. The whole affair ended with an incredible comeback, in the penultimate leg of the final race.

Having lived through this momentous event, camera in hand, with the simple intention of supplying a few lines of copy to yachting magazines, it was part and parcel of life's chance events. It's only later you realise how decisive such events are.

Pushing the adventure a little further

Until then I had only followed my teenage wishes: to sail, to race, all the while contributing to yachting magazines, between a few necessary visits to the faculty of Economic Science at Montpellier or Aix-en-Provence universities. I felt much more at home on a foredeck, handling a jib sheet, or perched 98ft (30m) up a mast inspecting a racing yacht's rigging.

It was impossible not to push the boundaries a little further. The Sea and See photo agency, founded by Daniel Allisy, sold my photo taken up the mast of *France III* for the cover of *Sail*, the top American sailing magazine of the time, in the issue that announced the Americans' historic defeat. Besides the pleasure of being published so prominently, the cheque that followed made me think about photography in a different light: it should be possible to turn it, if not into your main job, then into a parallel activity that would allow you to carry on sailing – either racing, doing deliveries or cruising. Big mistake: in these inspirational jobs, it is the job that takes the upper hand and the inspiration that is relegated to a subsidiary activity. If there's any time left …

The testing ground came two years later at sea off Fremantle, Western Australia, when the French Challenge went into bankruptcy, which meant I stayed put in Australia to cover the latest edition of the America's Cup instead of going back home. There, in the waves of

12-Metre
Australia II leads *Liberty*, in the mist, off the Newport coast during the final of the 1983 America's Cup, which will radically change the face of the most famous regatta in the world. Photo techniques at that time were still basic, but the main thing was just being there.

« I had the pleasure of beginning my career at a time when we took pictures, sent them to the lab and then met up with the crews at the yacht club bar without worrying about anything else. »

the Fremantle Doctor, the local wind thus named because it causes the scorching temperature of Western Australia to drop, the heavy 12-Metre yachts provided the ideal subject for the daily lessons in photography provided by Daniel Forster, Kaoru Soehata, Christian Février, Philip Plisson and other luminaries of maritime photography at the time.

The never-ending editing sessions on communal light boxes, where we checked the colour slides we had had developed overnight in Sydney, enabled me to learn the tricks of the trade. That meant discovering that, when you are on the same boat photographing the same scene, some take better pictures than others; they see things better or in a different way; they snap a scene more quickly or more efficiently, and they do not miss their shots for whatever shameful technical reasons. It was a formative experience!

The ego, or a spirit of competition, comes into play at that point, forcing you to do better the next day. In addition, I learned that year to work for agencies and the major dailies, to differentiate between news and magazine work, to respect deadlines and become reliable for the editorial staff rather than pointlessly easy-going. I even managed eventually to earn enough money to pay for one of those jewels without which you cannot be a true pro: a 300mm Nikon f/2.8. A wonder, a gem, a dream machine that gives you the feeling of having finally grown up. It was an illusion, no doubt, but it came with another lesson: you must never scrimp on equipment, because you are always asking yourself why it was that you waited so long (financial reasons aside) before equipping yourself with top-of-the-range cameras and lenses that, even if they don't make all the difference, at least enable you to match the competition on an equal footing.

And if novice photographers imagine this expenditure is a single, large investment at the start of their career, I'm sorry to say this is only the start of a continuous and long-term outlay.

Three jobs at once

Since then, photography has moved from the era of silver film and manual cameras to the era of digital files and automated cameras; it has seen the widespread use of ever longer and lighter telephoto lenses, the advent of autofocus and stabilised optics, increasingly small computer chips, which allow cameras to process more and more data and produce finer and finer pictures, the inclusion of video in SLR cameras, of immediate visualisation and of instantaneous transmission. Not to mention post-production, a term that was of no concern to photographers until the beginning of this century.

I had the pleasure of beginning my career at a time when we took pictures, sent them to the lab and then met up with the crews at the yacht club bar without worrying about anything else. Editing was for tomorrow or even later if it was a weekend or an exotic location trip, and it was the agencies' job to distribute the photographs. Nowadays we do all three jobs ourselves on the same day, sometimes at sea on a press boat or from the sky in a helicopter: the photographer's job (taking the shot itself), the lab's (the post-production process, which consists of processing and captioning the images) and the agency's (editing, putting the pictures online and distributing them via the Internet). We have become a hundred times more efficient and take up less room since abandoning the cubic metres of slides it is so difficult to get rid of, and we are certainly greener after the demise of those chemical baths that ended up God knows where. Nowadays, photographers

Wings
The use of rigid wings revolutionises the world of racing. Their transparency is an aesthetic blessing that completely changes the image of the sail and gives it a futuristic look.

work alone in a corner and are the last to leave the press room. You even find them sometimes the next morning with the shape of their computer's keys imprinted on their forehead because they have fallen asleep on the job …

Sailing, both racing and cruising, has developed enormously in the past 30 years too. It has witnessed the birth of racing multihulls, hulls with foils, self-furling gear, the staggering progress of electronic equipment and deck fittings, the Vendée Globe race, the birth of the classic yacht restoration movement, as well as three more generations of sailors. The great ocean pioneers of Tabarly's day have given way to ambitious young sailors who think in terms of their career and sponsorship and launch themselves into the Vendée Globe or the Volvo Ocean Race as though they were weekend outings. Weather forecasting and long-distance communications have improved massively, and the position-fixing of yachts even more so.

The sails of top racing yachts are not just made of sophisticated composite materials but of rigid wings, the crew wear helmets and it has become harder and harder to keep up with the boats in order to photograph them – so much so that photo shoots in helicopters have become the norm. Will still pictures in future be taken from high-definition videos filmed by satellite, from which we merely choose the best moments? Will we be replaced by drones? Presumably it's only a matter of time and method before anyone on the planet can choose a video online without a (by now redundant) photographer intercepting between them and reality.

But we are not quite there yet. Take advantage of the symbiotic marriage between photography and beautiful paper while you can: it's likely that this pleasure will also soon disappear, or at the very least become very scarce indeed …

Gilles Martin-Raget

Flying the nest . . .

Hike out!
Almost capsizing, this apprentice sailor, already wearing a helmet like his heroes of the America's Cup, is getting acquainted with the raw forces that govern a sailboat's equilibrium. Ease the mainsail a bit, lad!

Dinghy sailing is not as easy as it looks. Nothing is more important than the good health of this bobbing, bubbling world, which inspires young novices and Olympic champions alike.

Come on, let's go. Climb on board, lower the centreboard, trim the sails and let the music begin! Even though novices, both young and not so young, can now choose how they make their first encounter with the sea and boats, dinghy sailing is often the first stage in learning how to sail. Generally this initial experience takes place at a club and on an Optimist, a sort of soapbox with a spritsail, which has inspired thousands of kids across several generations to go sailing. That said, the windsurfer and now the kitesurfer allow the newbie to take a more appealing shortcut than the inevitable soaking sessions in store for those who go down the classic route. Attitudes to sailing have undeniably changed massively as the popularity of windsurfing has increased. Whole generations have been able to short-circuit the traditional dinghy sailing channels and have abandoned dinghy sailing forever, preferring the board's ease of use, its portability and, for the more daring, its speed and ability to jump over waves.

But dinghy sailing offers the most direct understanding of the forces at work when a boat is sailing. The power generated by the wind, its transmission through the sails and rigging, the behaviour of the hull as it heels over and then moves forward, the effect of the centreboard allowing you to sail in a straight line, the action of the rudder blade, which enables you to turn, the acceleration brought about by a fair wind, and sometimes capsizing because everything has not been properly coordinated. This discovery is truly fascinating, especially at a time when most things need a motor or electricity to work. In sailing, you move forward in silence – and this is nothing short of magic!

It's not surprising, then, that dinghy sailing at large still attracts many people who have not been through the sailing school programmes.

To counter the all-out attack from windsurfers of all kinds, dinghies have become lighter, faster, more sporty and also more unstable. Witness the 49er, which has become the most exhilarating and demanding class in the Olympic Games and which is a springboard for the most talented helm and crew to compete in professional races such as the America's Cup.

Everyone wants to fly

Sports catamarans, in the style of the great, pioneering Hobie Cat, have also contributed to the vitality of dinghy sailing. They are capable of exhilarating speeds, enabling sailors to cover greater distances, and have inspired the creation of mass participation events, with some events having 300 starters, and long-distance sailing raids lasting several days.

Better still: nowadays dinghies can fly. The mighty International Moth has enjoyed impressive success among seasoned sailors. Nowadays, the whole world wants to fly! Boards, kites, dinghies, sports catamarans. The principle is simple: once up on its foils, any floating machine becomes instantly faster because friction is reduced to the absolute minimum. It becomes a veritable turbo machine. Once out of the water, the machine's stability increases because it is higher than the waves, and the air flowing on the sails becomes more effective, accelerating the advantages of this virtuous circle. You just have to be careful not to break the delicate equilibrium or you'll be brutally returned to the world of full immersion …

The principle of foils is not a new one. Eric Tabarly was the first to try to lift a multihull out of the water. He first tested a model based on a Tornado catamaran before applying the principle to his foiling trimaran

Gotcha!
The man in a red cap perched on an AC45 going full pelt and giving a flick to the dinghy's sail is none other than Murray Jones, a Kiwi legend of the America's Cup. The blonde-haired young man on the 470, already dreaming of the Olympic Games, is his son. Kiwi racers never miss an opportunity to motivate the younger generations …

Paul Ricard, the first boat to beat the transatlantic record held for 75 years by the three-masted schooner *Atlantic*, skippered by Charlie Barr. Afterwards, racing multihulls tested the advantages of curved centreboards. Alain Thébault's *L'Hydroptère* beat several records, and the America's Cup multihulls have popularised the concept. The 2016 Olympic Games in Rio de Janeiro will see the Nacra 17, a double mixed sports catamaran fitted with curved boards, adopted as an Olympic class, which will enable sailors to go even faster.

The honour of representing one's country

Because it is, of course, the prospect of medals that motivates all top-level dinghy sailors. And what a tough vocation it is ... Years of training, thousands of miles travelling between one event and the next, days and days of hard work to gain a few centimetres here and there in the face of stiff competition, physical discipline in order to stay on top form, hundreds of hours spent studying tactics, strategy and communications – and all repeated for several years before you can even hope to be selected for the Olympic Games and have the honour of representing your country.

The Olympic Games remain an extraordinary event, even for the most dedicated champions. It's that special alchemy – produced by the combination of a high level of technical excellence, the enormous pressure of performing for your country, and the attention of friends and family, coaches and national delegations – which make the Olympic Games a test apart from all others. There you will see favourites crack up and disintegrate on a daily basis, or complete outsiders winning a race, soaring 120 per cent above their normal level during the crucial two weeks. There's nothing more moving than the presentation ceremony, those few seconds engraved on the memory of the medal winners for all eternity in gold, silver or bronze.

From the photographic point of view, dinghy sailing means you have to wet your wet weather gear, or rather your wetsuit. You have to be close to the action, therefore low on the water and on a sufficiently small boat to be able to approach the crews without bothering them. It's difficult to take pictures on board, especially when there's a breeze, although the advent of small waterproof sports cameras is revolutionising this practice. These can be set up anywhere, even on the sailors themselves. There's nothing more tricky than trying to capture those events that group all the races on the same stretch of water, such as the great weeks of Hyères, Kiel or Medemblik. With several classes racing at the same time, it's impossible to shoot them all in one day, which sometimes leads to frustrating choices. It's not much better at the Olympics, although the 'medal races' have clarified matters somewhat as they are raced one at a time! Another difficulty is the strict constraints imposed by security, which mean the players are only accessible after the races in a mixed area dedicated to interviews.

Star
One of the oldest racing keelboats still in operation and capable of gliding like a young 'un when in the hands of experts like Xavier Rohart and Pascal Rambeau. Seen here during a workout in the Bay of Cannes.

The school of life

Boys and girls who become passionate about sailing don't choose the easy route. They learn to fight against the forces of nature – with frostbite and the slap of the spray for good measure – and to create a space for themselves among a fleet of rivals who have the same equipment and chances as them on the starting line. Character-building stuff!

Future champions
(top and above) The Open BIC is an upgraded version of the ubiquitous Optimist, which allows the more talented to sail a less stable, faster and more modern-looking dinghy.

Girl power!
(right) Reserved for the best female racers in the world, and also for the most dynamic, the 49erFX is an only slightly more restrained version of the 49er, which will make its Olympic debut during the 2016 Rio Games. A real tippy propelled by a huge sail with a zero tolerance for errors.

Waves
There is always somewhere close to home to go and get windswept. Windsurfers start to surf when most other boats return to port and go exactly where the waves are the biggest and wildest.

Fun and speed

Windsurfing – funboard, waves, races, slaloms, speed records, and now kite surfing – it's incredible what the sport has brought to sailing by making it more dynamic, but also by diverting entire generations away from more conventional sailing.

Champions
(top) Antoine Albeau (left), multi-world champion, and Alexandre Caizergues (right), two formidable athletes who sail all year round and go faster than the rest, whatever type of board they have beneath their feet.

Cardio workout
(above) Olympic-style surfboard racing is a very demanding sport. Athletes have to permanently 'pump' to create an increase in power, especially at the start line.

470
(above) This tireless dinghy, conceived by André Cornu, continues to serve as the workhorse for thousands of enthusiasts of all abilities. The best school bench from which to learn how to receive a face-full of spray.

Olé!

By its very nature, a dinghy has a tendency to capsize, whether on one hull or two. Without a keel, it is the crew who balance out the boat's force and stability. As the tendency when racing is to sit to leeward, the slightest error can be costly. Especially when faced with a strong breeze.

18ft Skiffs
(left) The 'Skiffs', invented in Sydney bay, still feature among the world's most acrobatic sailboats. Sailed by a three-member crew, they fly on the water or even above it. If things go wrong, it can take quite a while to put everything back in place and get going again …

Mixed crews
(right) The Nacra 17 is the latest craze for mixed crews. The lady at the helm, the man on the trapeze (or vice-versa, depending on individual physical size).

Fly, dinghy, fly!

Welcome to the future. Built in a powerful manner and with simple yet intelligent solutions to help the dinghy fly, the moth has revolutionised lightweight dinghies, in practice as well as in appearance. These new dragonflies sail at lightning-fast speeds and without a sound, without spray and apparently effortlessly, too. Absolute dynamite!

Staying in the air
(above, top and opposite page) Just like on a surfboard, the hardest bit is getting going, and then coming back. A Moth only works when it's flying, and splashes about like an ugly duckling when at a standstill. The transition between the two states requires a certain amount of *savoir-faire*. And then comes the time to bear away, which is always delicate, and the time to gybe without capsizing, which is even harder.

Raids

(right) Many sailors appreciate the long-distance formula, which allows the blend of sport with the pleasure of discovering new stretches of water and sometimes rather exotic sailing conditions. The sports catamaran requires a lot of skill to avoid letting the breeze force you nose first into the water. Serious sensations await you!

Tornado

The success of sports catamarans is in no way waning, even if the Tornado (left), by far the most powerful model, was brutally evicted from the Olympic Games with no warning. The Nacra 17, which replaces it (above), is much more acrobatic thanks to its curved foils.

Gold
(far left) During the awards ceremony, all eyes are on the winners, sometimes becoming national heroes, as was the case of the windsurfer Yin Jian. She was the first Chinese national to obtain a gold medal in sailing (Beijing 2008).

Silver
(bottom left) Devastated for having missed out on the ultimate victory by a few metres in the final medal race. Julien Bontemps, silver medallist in RS:X windsurfing at Beijing in 2008.

Bronze
(top left) A medal round the neck, but tears nonetheless, of joy, sadness, exhaustion, emotion. Guillaume Florent, bronze medallist in the Finn at Beijing in 2008.

Sir Ben
(opposite page) The Brit Sir Ben Ainslie has won Olympic sailing gold four times and silver once, an exceptional achievement.

Olympics: all or nothing

The amount of pressure that sailing champions are under during the Olympic Games, even if lessened through years of practice competing at the highest level, can either crush or thrill the competitors. With the exception of the start or finish of the Vendée Globe, there are no more moving moments, no feelings more intense, in joy as well as sorrow, than the Olympic Games medal ceremonies. For those who miss out on the podium, this can be a horrible fate, as it obliterates, in an instant, the years of training, struggle and hope. In the best case scenario, some can hope to attend the next Olympic Games, and so re-enlist for another four years, while for others it will be the end of a career with a slightly bitter aftertaste.

Creeks in Corsica or the Balearic Islands?

The choice of cruising areas in the Mediterranean is so vast that one could quite happily sail here forever. The western basin alone hides priceless treasures, with destinations along the Spanish, French and Italian coasts, not to mention Corsica, the Balearic Islands, the islands scattered along the foot of Italy, Sicily, and the Maghreb coast of North Africa. If you include Greece and Turkey, a whole other universe opens up before you.

If I had to chose one place? It would without a doubt be the Strait of Bonifacio, the stretch of water separating the south coast of Corsica, where you can always shelter from strong (and sometimes very strong!) winds, and the maze of islands of the Maddalena Archipelago off the north coast of Sardinia. You could spend days anchoring here and there without ever coming back to the same spot, and end up by fetching up at the fantastic site of Bonifacio to sample the incomparable Corsican cuisine.

Corsica
(above) Spring mooring in the Lavezzi Islands, south Corsica. The months of June and September are exquisite all over the Mediterranean, but even more so here than elsewhere.

Balearics
Historic citadel of Port Mahon in Minorca (top left), boats and fisherman's shelter in Formentera (above), the Balearics offer a unique place of discovery for lovers of cruising.

Calanques
This could be anywhere in the Mediterranean, where limestone and turquoise blue waters often go hand in hand.
This very private mooring destination is at Loule, at the foot of the Marseille calanques.

Île de Riou
(previous double-page spread) Many moorings are starting to be regulated to avoid overpopulation, like here in Monasterio, which is located by the Île de Riou in the Calanques National Park.

Sperone
A golf course, a beach, a white sandy isthmus, the island of Piana to the left, Lavezzi a bit further afield and the Sardinian archipelago within a bow's reach, pushed along by a gentle westerly breeze. In other words, all the beauty of the Strait of Bonifacio in a single image.

Inshore racing

A crowded start line

Charge!
Bows wedged in with millimetres to spare at the Youth America's Cup starting line, a race reserved for crew members under the age of 23 and who race on AC45s propelled by rigid wings. No room for any more boats, not even a monohull!

'Inshore racing' is a blanket term for any event in which you race under sail around three buoys and then go home at night. Well, not right away – only after the obligatory stop at the club bar, where you can relive the whole race. As for the rest, it's total war!

Racing is above all a social sport, which consists of proving to your peers that you are the fastest in the bay, the region, the continent or the world. All that remains is to choose the vessel. It could be a monotype or a maxi yacht, monohull or multihull, a yacht that will accommodate a crew of between three and 30, an extreme racer or a more modest yacht that will do for cruising a little later – a vast range of possibilities is available. You can sail around permanent navigation buoys or temporary race buoys, around islands and rocks, or from one harbour to the next. But some things remain the same: there is always a crowded start, there are changes of pace depending on the strength and direction of the wind, and there is an arrival. There are rules governing rights of way, and juries to enforce them. There are race committees that organise everything and will cancel racing if the weather is too bad. And you must always end up in the club bar, no matter what!

'Water! Water!' is the cry. As if the sea isn't big enough for everyone, sailors have to fight over one little patch of water! This is what happens, though, at the start of every race. It is somewhat bizarre. Can you imagine the runners of a 100-metre race all starting in a bundle? Or Formula 1 drivers rushing ahead without having prearranged positions on the starting grid?

In sailing, there is none of that. Instead, there is an invisible line between a committee boat and a buoy, and it's up to whoever can clear a path and grab the best position – ie, the place with the best angle to the wind – and judge their speed just right so they cross the line just as the starting gun is fired. The helms have few weapons at their disposal, apart from the right of way rules, a strong sense of 'time over distance',

and perfect command of their crew and their boat, as well as strong vocal chords!

The emergence of the latest trends

The last ten years have seen yacht racing evolve to fit the times. Traditionally, there was one race a day around the coastline or three buoys. But the sportsmen wanted more sport, and organisers now have to maximise the sailing season. There are several races in a day, often shorter than before, with straight upwind and downwind courses. It is intense, technically demanding and makes the whole thing very punchy and active, placing a greater importance on the starts. The windward-leeward course has become the norm, often with extra 'gates' you have to sail through to avoid the dangerous pile-ups that occur when boats sail too close to the buoys.

The latest trend is 'stadium sailing', which takes place close to terra firma so that spectators, members of the media and sponsors' guests in the VIP enclosures can experience the action at close quarters. The Olympic Games have paved the way in this, under pressure from the International Olympic Committee, which sees sport purely as a television opportunity. The global audience must be able to understand and be captivated by something, or it's out. In keeping with this dictum, the sailing fraternity came up with the concept of 'medal races' for the 2008 Olympic Games in Beijing. The first round is treated as racing trials, with only the ten best sailors making it through to the final race, and the finishing order of the final race decides who gets the medals. It's a drastic system that was not received with unanimity among the sailors, who were not used to such an all-or-nothing approach.

Heavyweights
Nothing is more spectacular than the large and very heavy monohulls and a nice Mistral breeze to brighten up the waterfront at Les Voiles de Saint-Tropez. Anticipation, care and skill at the tiller are all vital on the starting line, without which one could easily make a large hole in the carbon hulls. Always remember: boats don't have any brakes …

Drastic changes

The 34th America's Cup in San Francisco in 2013 went even further by creating a kind of race track sailed by wing-sail catamarans. Firstly: the preparation time before the start gun was reduced to a strict minimum, only three minutes instead of the usual ten. Secondly: instead of having to beat into the wind after the start, the boats sailed at full speed with the wind on the side for a very short leg towards the first, hotly contested turn. It's a bit like car racing, except there are no brakes, and everyone is driving at full speed! The public, positioned on this first leg, is sure to get their money's worth (yes, you have to pay to watch nowadays …). Thirdly: the boundaries of the rectangular course are guarded by electronic sensors, which competitors must not cross on pain of penalty. This is to prevent them straying too far from one another, to ensure close contact and thus to make a spectacle of themselves. This system imposes high electronic requirements, as each boat must be equipped with a super-precise position-finder, and is best suited to fast yachts. Finally, with such super-precise position-finding, the refereeing can take place partly at a distance, and the many cameras on board operated by remote control enable the events to be transmitted directly to the world at large.

From the photographic point of view, it is during the inshore races that you can expect to take the most spectacular and varied images, because of the many different types of courses and boats, as well as the varied seascapes and weather conditions. One thing is essential: to be on a good motorboat that does not get too wet, skippered by a good pilot who will find the best position, generally near the buoys where the action is more intense, without disturbing the race in any way. It cannot be stressed enough how important a role the pilots of camera boats, and sometimes helicopters, play in the work of marine or yachting photographers. As for the equipment, a hand-held telephoto lens is indispensable for capturing the action on deck. In terms of size, the only limit is what you can carry (and pay for), but you could quite reasonably stretch to a 600mm lens with an extension, making it 1,200mm! Bigger than that, and you can only take pictures of clouds or waves, not of boats.

There's nothing better than a good race battled out in more than 25 knots of wind, even if committees (and competitors) are increasingly shy of firing the start gun in a strong breeze. The more contestants there are, the heavier the boats; the more wind there is, the bigger waves – and the bigger the spectacle!

Lightweights
When it is light, it flies, it glides, it goes very quickly and it drenches people, like this monotype Open 6.50 dayboat, following an exhilarating downwind leg during the International Nautical Week of Marseille.

One design

This is probably the best racing school one could imagine as everyone has the same equipment. As with the dinghy, a number of boats have been developed and have quickly become very popular, such as the Open 5.70 in France (left), or the Melges 20 in Italy (top right). The J24 (middle right) remains the most popular worldwide. His stable companion, the First Class 8 (bottom right) requires the least amount of concentration when facing the breeze …

Cruiser racing

It doesn't exactly grab the headlines, but it is still a passion for thousands of enthusiasts. The Cowes Week Sailing Regatta in the UK, the Spi Ouest-France Intermarché at Trinité-sur-Mer, the Key West Race Week in Florida, the Big Boat Series in San Francisco and the Kieler Woche in Germany are all unmissable events for those who only attend a few races every year. Not forgetting the innumerable club regattas or local championships that allow those with a 'normal' boat, which can be used both for racing and cruising, to have fun as well.

Pro level

At the top of the scale, the TP52 is a race prototype conceived from a 'box rule', a restriction gauge that limits the minimum and maximum sizes of the boats. Wealthy owners, helped by their commercial sponsors, entrust professional racers with their jewel. Result: the races are extreme. The boats are simple and solid, which means that race starts can have up to 30 knots of wind, a phenomenon that is becoming scarce in the world of racing.

Full speed ahead!
(left) A furious downwind leg for these TP52s pushed by lovely summer Mistral winds in Marseille harbour.

One length, no more

(above) *Quantum*, the green-coloured TP52 being crossed by the American Terry Hutchinson, has priority. *Team New Zealand* (black and red) has to leave enough room for them to round the buoy. But Dean Barker, the Kiwi helmsman, won't give them an inch more than necessary …

One length, no less

(right) Competition can be fierce when every boat looks the same and goes at the same speed. To win, everything comes down to the start of the race. Then it's up to the tacticians to find the shortest route, and up to the crew members to avoid mistakes. Keep calm and carry on!

IACC
Initially conceived as a prize horse for the America's Cup professionals, the Class America (International America's Cup Class) is governed by a series of very strict technical rules that have served as the highest professional touchstone for nearly two decades. These machines are highly efficient to tackle headwinds, but are less exciting downwind due to their narrowness and lead keels, which weigh almost 20 tonnes.

Surf

(above) Match racing isn't a stroll in the park, but with a breeze it becomes sheer folly. Aggressiveness, nerves of steel, hyper-concentration, experience, reflexes, anticipation and outstanding crew timing are of the essence.

Match racing

Match racing is the highest form of sailing duels, which matches competitors against one of their opponents. What counts isn't necessarily to go quickly, but just to cross the finish line before the other contender. Originally conceived to train America's Cup crews between races, this type of merciless confrontation has progressively evolved into a real international circuit that brings together a dozen events, some of which have a substantial money prize. The boats certainly don't have an easy ride!

On the defence

(left) To stop their opponent from going past, the boat with the red and white spinnaker is allowed to send its challenger into headwinds without false airs and graces, and for as long as it chooses to. A radical defence manoeuvre.

Making contact

(right) Clashes, blows to the bow, impacts of all sorts, small holes and big dents are not rare in this type of race, even if they result in an immediate penalty given by the ever-present umpires in the thick of it on the water.

Starboard tack, king of the seas
The rules governing races change every four years when the Olympics come around, but the rule of 'Starboard tack, king of the seas' – in other words, starboard tack always has priority – remains the solid basis for decision-making. The other key rule, though not written down anywhere, requires giving way to very large yachts when we are just a tiny bit smaller …

It leans

(left) Like all other catamarans, an AC45 is most efficient when the windward hull lifts just a touch off the water. Easier said than done when you have a rigid wing as a motor, even with the likes of Dean Barker at the helm for *Team New Zealand*.

It jumps

(above) AC45s don't like to be close to others in rough seas, even if they are being led by the Australian multiple champion Darren Bundock supported by his *Oracle Team USA* crew.

And it drenches

(right) In the breeze, AC45s give their crews a good drenching, like the *Luna Rossa*, seen here in exceptionally choppy Neapolitan waters.

Nosedive
(top left) Bearing away is the most uncertain phase with an AC45 facing the breeze. One must keep up an even speed to make the most of the buoyancy of the two bows. Sometimes, though, this isn't enough to avoid disaster …

Transparency
(bottom left) Venice is the backdrop for the maiden voyage of an AC45 in the Youth America's Cup colours, reserved for young sailors. Given the kind of bullfighting taking place and the sponsor's colours, this picture could just as easily have been taken in Spain.

Sainte-Dévote
(right) Passing the race's first buoy for an AC45 at Newport is not unlike passing the Sainte-Dévote bend in the Monaco F1 Grand Prix race. We never know who will come out first, or who will remain in one piece …

AC45

The AC45s were created in 2011 to train the America's Cup crews on the new methods of handling catamarans with rigid wings. There have been spectacular races, which have allowed crews to try out the new Cup rules in situ. In the breeze, crews are subjected to a gruelling physical pace, and battle permanently not to be the victim of the instability of the platforms propelled by over-powerful wings. The spectators, on the other hand, have a whale of a time watching!

Italy and the Adriatic, of course!

Forza Italia! Italians are born sailors. Their country is surrounded by water, and they live on a large island. Apart from possibly Greece, there are few countries that offer as many cruising opportunities or as many delightful seascapes. There is nothing hostile or wild here, just gentleness, humanity, and the knowledge that everything here is the product of history, culture and knowledge. This is not ostentatious, it is a fact, a given. The sea is there, has always been there, and people have always used it. They know that if the sea gets too wild, they will just wait for it to calm down. Their boats have adapted to this, they are beautiful, and no one knows how to handle them like a *marinaio*. It is not for nothing that Genoa, Naples, Venice, Capri and Syracuse, as well as Portofino, Porto Venere and Ventotene are in Italy. If you fancy getting lost in a maze of islands, you only have to cross the Adriatic and head to the Kornati Islands. *Che bello!*

Sicily
(above) ORMA trimarans' regatta, with the San Lorenzo cathedral in Trapani, on the western tip of Sicily in the foreground. A maritime town where the Norman explorers dropped anchor many moons ago, close to the magical archipelago of the Aegadian Islands.

Boot
From Portofino (top left) on the Ligurian coast of the Gulf of Genoa to the island village of Tribunj (above) in Croatia, the range of possible destinations around the Adriatic is absolutely infinite.

Liguria
Classic rigging in Imperia, Liguria, which welcomes the best in classic sailing every other year. It is also one of the main Italian destinations when travelling from the Côte d'Azur. A change of scenery guaranteed.

Serenissima
(previous double-page spread) Yes, it is possible to sail on the Venice's Grand Canal, and even race. Perched at the top of the Adriatic, La Serenissima is one of the most beautiful and rewarding destinations to visit when cruising in the Mediterranean.

Kornati archipelago
To each his corner of the Kornati Islands, which make up this Croatian archipelago. Shade from the trees might be rare but it is offset by the slow and mild pace of local life.

Manœuvres

The empire of the foredeck

Number one
At the very edge of the
foredeck and just above
the threatening bow wave,
being a bowman is both
physical and demanding.

Welcome aboard. Take care not to bump your head, do not disturb the crew, behave yourself and say nothing. Lower your head when the boat goes about, and do not interfere with the lines. Love racing? You will be well catered for here!

Not all jobs on racing yachts have the same status. Naturally the person at the helm is king of the race, the best known and the most visible member of the crew. Usually also given the title of skipper, they are regarded as magicians, capable of making a boat go faster and higher into the wind than anyone else. They are blessed with a certain aura that allows them to demand the best from their troops in the worst conditions. Never more at ease than when sailing a boat, their real talent is revealed in the spirit with which they approach the start lines. Their heavily laden trophy shelves speak for themselves.

They are closely followed in the pecking order by the tactician, another species apart from the human race, who speaks the language of the winds and who can detect imperceptible changes better than anyone else. They can sense the subtle rocking motion no one else noticed, which allows the boat to gain a precious few dozen metres. Their skill is a little magical too, as the decisions they take are often governed by intuition, by an innate flair, by the experience they have gleaned sailing the world's waters. They know everything there is to know about racing rules and, with one hand on the protest flag and an eye on the competition, they will shout to make sure their right of way is recognised. On the other hand, unlike other crew members whose errors can often go unnoticed, everyone can see when a tactician makes a mistake, and it is up to them to defend the boat's honour should a protest be made against it. It's a job that is not without stress …

Then there is the sail trimmer, already a more technical job. They are entrusted with supplying the boat's power, and generally their job is deciding whether to add or reduce sail. Working in conjunction with the helm, they help to ease the pressure on the helm, to power up the boat or to sail more closely to the wind, depending on the prevailing tactics. They know the yacht's sail wardrobe and which sail is best suited to which wind, and can create the ideal aerodynamic shape by tweaking various lines. Sheet in hand, their eye fixed on the readings that show the strength and the angle of the wind, as well as the boat's speed and course, they are usually blessed with good brains and have to manage the grinders, the crew who operate the winches and who supply the necessary power when the boat is going about, gybing or changing sails.

The masters of manoeuvres

It would be an insult to those who operate the winches to regard them as just brawn, and to quantify their contribution in terms of mere power. Not only does their knowledge of how the sails work help both the trimmers and the helm, but being at the centre of the boat means they have a key position within the crew, a sort of driving belt between the 'cowboys' at the back and the 'Indians' at the front. For no one goes in front of the mast willingly!

Next, welcome to the world of the master sail-handler, the king of the fast headsail change, the emperor of the flying gybe and other sophisticated manoeuvres: the bowmen. Here a job well done is no joke. Anticipation, coordination, teamwork, swiftness, agility and even a taste for danger are the qualities required by these sailors. Unlike those at the back of the boat, they are first in line to face the might of the ocean and the dangerous forces unleashed by the foresails when they are released. Bowmen belong to a particular class of sailors who recognise and respect each other. They are in the thick of it during the

Timing
There can be no errors during countdown, which precedes the firing of the starting gun. One eye on the stopwatch, the other on the competition, the crew relies on the helmsman's talents to find the best spot on the starting line.

start line battles, and skippers rely on them to tell them when they are approaching the invisible line.

To earn the title of 'Number One' you must have practised all possible manoeuvres beforehand and know how to react when a sheet breaks, a sail is torn, an order is given too late, or there's a sudden change in the wind that means a sail must be changed urgently. Inevitably, the bowmen are also the favourite subject of yachting photographers, because their dynamic role puts them in the most perilous positions and makes them much more photogenic than the rest of the crew, sitting around the boat.

Reduction of personnel

Unfortunately, most racing boats are nowadays equipped with gennakers, which are infinitely easier to handle than the more unstable spinnakers. Roller-furling sails, the shapes of which have made enormous progress, do away with about a dozen sails and the sail-changing operations that go with them. It's been a long time since any racing boat has taken in a reef, at least in inshore races.

Worst of all, the America's Cup multihulls have effectively eliminated all deck work. These devilish machines go so fast and the apparent wind is so high, that there's no point in bothering with downwind sails. Races are so short that it's unthinkable to change foresails; you keep the same sails up from start to finish. Besides, there is not even a foredeck any more, just a fairing that the crew are asked not to walk on in case they break it. It's a real disgrace. The crew have been reduced to turning handles to supply hydraulic energy, and it won't be long before the requirement to use human energy will disappear altogether, which will

spell the end of any crew. A skipper, a tactician, and some push-button trimmers will be all that's needed. Life's a bitch …

From the photographic point of view, to be allowed on a boat just to take pictures is one of the most exhilarating aspects of the job. You are the heart of the action, going at full speed, with all the excitement of the race in front of you. You need to stay calm when you're on deck, especially when taking pictures of what is happening in front of the mast. Space is limited and you might get elbowed quite a lot. Watch out for the flogging sails and sheets, and for sudden waves. You have to make sure you are in a good position before the manoeuvre starts as everything happens in a flash, and always avoid getting in the way of the crew, otherwise you'll get black looks and would be strongly advised to retire to the back. Watertight equipment is obligatory in windy weather, and minimum movements in calm weather. You have to blend in with the crew, respect their priorities and not walk around the deck like an elephant, otherwise there will be no next time.

The winchmen
Hoisting of the mainsail aboard the TP52 *Matador*. The winchmen act as the crew's heart. They have to know how to develop brute force or help to regulate the sails with finesse. A vigorous and rhythmic heartbeat is essential.

Composite sails
(above and opposite right) The concept of flaking a sail has lost its meaning since the introduction of composite sails that are as stiff as a board and covered in a plastic film to facilitate the air flow. It's therefore impossible to bring the material onto the deck if the sail hasn't been completely depowered first.

The drop
(left) The dousing of large spinnakers or gennakers, which measure several hundred square metres, remains a special moment during a race for all crew members, but especially those of a maxi-monohull. This manoeuvre is impossible to carry out alone and so must be a team effort. The coordination must be perfect because if the wind picks up in the sail, problems can become serious, very quickly.

Team spirit

The art of manoeuvring is based on techniques that have been developed by crews in order to master physical forces that are stronger than they are. It is necessary to work alone, in pairs, in threes or more depending on the situation. The size of the boat and of its rigging only serve to make the problems all the more delicate. The amount of effort grows exponentially, which makes the management of team numbers and their coordination all the more crucial.

Bowsprits
(right) Large yachts with bowsprits, such as the immense *Adela*, only serve to add to the difficulties crews are faced with due to the narrowness of their workspace and the instability linked to moving on a net. The only solution to manage the foresails: all hands on deck, especially the big, strong ones!

Gybe set in Kiwi drop

There isn't a single way, but rather a dozen ways of sending a gennaker and spinnaker on the attack on the downwind leg, and just as many ways, if not more, of lowering it a few minutes later. The ballet that unfolds on the foredeck must be choreographed down to the centimetres and seconds in order to avoid a major mess. If the rear cell (helmsman, navigator and tactician) warned everyone in advance, everything should go according to plan. But the uncertainties linked to race conditions mean that orders – or worse, disorders – can only be given at the last moment. For the front acrobats, it is best to anticipate all possible outcomes …

The rigging
(opposite page) Oh, aren't the small black carbon fibre spreaders pretty? You know, the ones that are just waiting for the chance to rip the spinnaker or gennaker during manoeuvres. On large yachts, while everything is going well, it's possible to remain in the race, but if a manoeuvre problem arises, the end of the race is never far away …

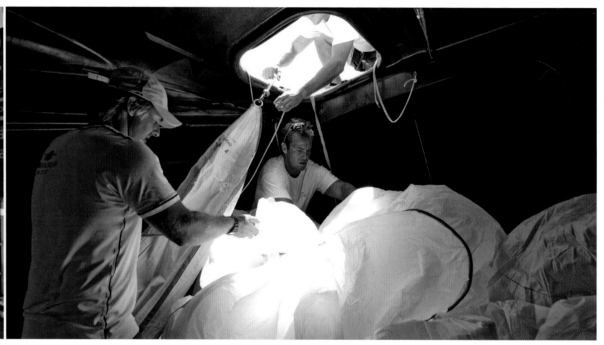

The pianist
Located at the bottom of the mast, the position of 'pianist' (from the name given to the battery of blockers that are available to them) is crucial in all manoeuvres as this is where the halyards and ropes are either stiffened (strained) or chocked (released), which allows the crew to set and sometimes tweak the sails. Very technical indeed.

The sail sewer
The role of sail sewer is not exactly the most glamorous, but it is definitely one of the most physical as it necessitates working and refolding the sails in a space that is as confined as it is reduced. The Anglo-Saxons gave people with this role the lovely nickname of 'mushroom', as they seem to develop in the humid conditions brought about by all that hard work and sweat!

(following double-page spread) A selection of bowman manoeuvres, or the art and manner of managing the most critical of situations when the sails do whatever they feel like.

Louis Vuitton Cup Series
(opposite and above) Contested during the winter in Dubai, when the sun was low on the horizon, the Louis Vuitton Cup Series in November 2010 will remain in the history books as the last race of the International America's Cup Class, and also as one of the most aesthetically pleasing that has ever been contested.

Lookout, do you see anything coming?

There have always been sailors perched in the rigging, but the time of looking for 'Land Ahoy!' or the enemy has long gone. The job is now to identify the gusts of wind that can help you win a race in calm weather, and most definitely to help the mainsail battens resume their correct position after each tack or gybe. With the help of a few kicks if necessary …

Impregnable views
(above and right) It is not necessarily the most fun job to spend hours attached by a harness at the top of a mast to watch the others racing, but what a great spot from which to follow the side by side duels between two maxis!

Athleticism

(top and above) The deck plan for the AC45 was designed to emphasise the crew's athletic qualities. Minimalist fittings, a trampoline that must be crossed with a central beam in the way, even the American all-stars had a rough time of it.

Fire hose

(left) Multihulls such as the AC45s always sail very quickly and send their wake to the middle of the trampoline with a lot of pressure. The quicker they go, the quicker and stronger the waves get. A real pleasure.

Wingsails

(right) Contrary to popular belief, a wingsail is easier to manage than a composite material mainsail, even if it gives much more power. The camber and general orientation are the only two variables, but they are crucial. On board an AC45, the wing controller, more than the skipper, has control of the boat's speed at his fingertips.

The Caribbean, from north to south

The good thing about the Caribbean is that there's something for everyone. You can enjoy the wildness of the Saint Blas Islands and Los Roques, the urban areas of Martinique, Guadeloupe, Antigua, St Bart's and Saint Martin, the isolation of St Kitts and Nevis, the authenticity of Dominica, or the perfectly delightful such as the Grenadines. Cuba, Puerto Rico and the Bahamas promise delights and discoveries for those who take a northerly route. The wind blows generally across the route, and even if the narrows and headlands are sometimes a bit rough, the mildness of the air and the sea, the sight of a flying fish skimming across the water, or of a frigatebird gliding between two towering cumulus clouds, will make the time pass more quickly. Naturally it's a bit crowded in winter, you have to watch out for the cyclone season in summer, and the sea's quite rough all the year round but, in general, this is one of the most beautiful cruising destinations in the world. It's not by chance that charter fleets have sprung up here more quickly and more effectively than elsewhere. To be enjoyed without moderation.

Gum tree canoes
(above) The tradition of racing gum tree canoes and round skiffs is still alive and well in the West Indies, especially in Martinique.

Coconut trees
(top left and above) From the British Virgin Islands to the Bahamas, from Roques to Antigua, like all other tropical destinations, the coconut tree is the symbol of a nonchalant lifestyle, lulled by the rhythm of the trade winds.

Tobago Cays
There aren't that many places in the Caribbean where you can sail on a turquoise water basin. The Tobago Cays lagoon in the Grenadines is a notable exception that is well worth a visit: a beautiful prime anchoring spot.

Sam Blas Islands
(previous double-page spread) Located close to Panama, the San Blas archipelago is a national park inhabited by some 50,000 Kuna Indians who have refused mass tourism for decades. This maze of flat coral islands remains one of the most unspoilt places in the Caribbean Sea.

Marie-Galante

A touch of turquoise blue, a splattering of coconut green, a dash of white from the waves' surf, a lovely trade wind, a desert island close by, two bows gathering speed and the wind in your sails, what more could one ask for when heading for a dream break in Marie-Galante?

Perils of the sea
Topsy-turvy

Without a paddle
The AC45 China Team skipper is none other than the Australian champion Mitch Booth, one of the most decorated multihull racers in the world. His boat capsizing in front of the America's Cup World Series crowd in Plymouth in 2011 is absolutely guaranteed to cause a stir.

Perils of the sea is a term used for a huge list of accidents, breakages and other misfortunes that can befall those who venture out to sea. For these unfortunate sailors, the range of possibilities is infinite.

Soaking, capsizing, blown-out equipment, sheared lines, sails ripped or dragging in your wake, broken spars, sheared rudder blade, broken-down engine, leaking hydraulics, electrical shorts and even a lost keel – nothing will be spared the unfortunate sailor. Sailing is, after all, an equipment-driven sport that racing pushes to its limits, and sometimes beyond its limits. Apart from the America's Cup and a few well-funded offshore projects that have the resources to test the dozens of rules that govern a particular class's design and construction, the material strength of a sailing yacht is usually tested out at sea. Designers and equipment manufacturers impose wide safety margins, but it's extremely difficult to calculate beforehand the brutal forces imposed by a boat-breaking sea, not to mention the ageing of the materials in this hostile environment.

Theoretical knowledge is one thing but putting it into practice is another. Boatbuilding is an area fraught with difficulties, which sometimes result in breakages and misery, although these are becoming less with the increased use of exotic fibres for hulls, sails and deck fittings. Go figure why a steel keel snaps in two or why a hull that has already sailed around the world several times suddenly decides to break up. Dismastings are always spectacular, and rarely explained, and the way jury rigs are set up is an amazing test of ingenuity.

Carrying out repairs at sea is always a headache, given the meagre resources available on board in terms of equipment, space and manpower. The uncontested champion in this category is Yves Parlier, who competed in the 2000 Vendée Globe race. After breaking his mast, he rebuilt it out of carbon fibre in an isolated part of New Zealand using just the equipment he had on board. To keep within the race rules, he refused any outside assistance and went on to finish the race – though not before having to invent new ways of feeding himself and drinking when his cupboard ran dry. It was an astonishing feat of resourcefulness and determination!

One thing is certain: when a breakage occurs, sailors have their hands full, because it's rarely an isolated problem. It's more likely that one problem will create other problems, thus unleashing a terrible spiral that often ends in disaster. At best, the boat might lose a bit of momentum, do badly in the race, and eventually have to drop out altogether. At worst it might mean shipwreck, having to abandon the yacht and putting many lives in danger.

Confronting the worst …

Going to sea means being aware of these risks. Nature can be hostile, and things that break are always dangerous. A flogging sail can knock someone out, like a boom that is out of control and catches the head of a careless or novice crew. Loose lines can burn your hands or even break limbs if they get tangled around you. Below decks, you can bump your head or burn yourself on boiling water.

But the worst scenario is a man overboard. Yes, you can go back and pick up the poor wretch, as happened with solo sailor Alain Gautier, who was rescued by one of his rivals in the Figaro race, and Florence Arthaud, who was saved by her mobile phone while she was floundering in the sea off Corsica. Both accidents took place out at sea, and both rescues were miracles. No miracle happened when the young crew of the Volvo Ocean Race 2006 lost a man in the middle of the Atlantic, found his body too late, and had to haul it back on board and keep it there until the end of the race. What could be worse?

Boom!
An unavoidable penalty for these three TP52s during a race in Marseille at the end of what could be described as a hopeless situation.

Even if sailing is an infinitely less dangerous sport than mountaineering, death at sea is always a painful occurence. Everyone was shocked by the death of Eric Tabarly and of respected sailors such as Alain Colas, Loïc Caradec and Paul Vatine. More recently, the death of the British Olympic champion Andrew Simpson, when the catamaran *Artemis* capsized in San Francisco Bay, is a terrible, awful reminder that the worst can happen on any racing yacht.

And celebrating the best!

But the best can also happen, and good things sometimes come from adversity. The Vendée Globe race in 2000 was a veritable treasure trove of life-affirming stories, such as the experience of Raphaël Dinelli, who found himself riding his upturned vessel while he waited for help to come, and of Tony Bullimore who spent three days inside his capsized and keel-less yacht, while he waited for help in the middle of the Southern Ocean. The Australian Navy crew who reached Bullimore's wreck and knocked on the hull to see if there was any life on board, sure that there would be none, still dance for joy when they remember the moment they heard a voice call back to them. These stories of miraculous rescues, of daring manoeuvres by Russian cargo ships – it's always a Russian, Polish or Korean ship, God knows why! – and of mutual support between seafaring people, are happily more numerous than tales of misfortune. While some misguided people point to the high cost of these rescues and the dangers the sailors who have accidents while sailing for their own pleasure put their rescuers in, this tradition of assisting others who are in distress is one of the highest principles perpetuated by the seafaring world.

From the photographic point of view, you must be ready, with all your reflexes on high alert. You can anticipate problematic situations, such as when several boats reach a buoy at the same time, or if the wind blows very strongly, which often heralds breakages. The difficulty often lies in not being frightened by the scenario and being able to carry on photographing it. How you manage your feelings in good as well as bad moments is a very personal question for each photographer. Let's just say that in maritime photography, a certain amount of restraint is essential. It's better to miss a photo opportunity if you feel too close to the sailors in distress, than the opposite.

Crack!
(opposite page) Goodbye beautiful composite material mainsail on this 60ft ORMA trimaran during the 2003 Lorient Regatta. Next stop: the port and sailmakers …

The keel …

(top right) … *France 2*
went to join the bottom of
the Pacific Ocean off San
Diego in 1995. If capsizing
in a multihull is not
desirable but just about
manageable, to lose one's
keel when in a monohull is
just not on …

Running aground

(middle right) It isn't rare
to run aground at Cowes,
where the current forces
you to tack close to land to
gain some ground. Some
crews are a bit too daring
and run aground in the
sand. When the boat's
structure gives way due to
the shock, the rest of the
operations become a little
more complicated …

Breaking up

(bottom right) Boats
breaking in two are
fortunately quite rare,
but it has happened on
a few occasions to some
America's Cup IACCs
due to their extreme
construction, as was the
case for *Young America*
during the Louis Vuitton
Cup 2000, held in
Auckland.

Trawling

(opposite left) This is what
happens when you badly
manage dousing the
spinnaker: the wind picks up
in your sails; the sail goes in
the water, which takes over
with a lot more force. From
this point on, there is only
one solution: stop the boat
and pick up the fragments of
what remains.

Dismasting

One rig, just one rig! There is potentially a spare mast ashore ready
to be installed on the Italian IACC *+39*, but there is definitely a lot
more work ahead for the team in the coming hours.

Sawed
During the spectacular dismasting of the giant trimaran *USA 17* in San Diego in 2009, the mast fell backwards on the traveller tack, the most rigid part of the boat. The rigging was out of use but the platform remained intact. If it had broken a brace or a float while falling, the history of the America's Cup would have changed forever.

Tidying up
(opposite) A dismasting incident is always traumatic as, after the explosion of the piece breaking, one never really knows where the rigging is going to drop. The advantage of a multihull, such as Michel Desjoyeaux's *Géant*, is that there is room to work to put things back to rights. You first have to de-rig the sail and retrieve the carbon tube sections, possibly towing to port the sections that are already in the water.

Complicated
Harder to manage: the top section of the mast breaks. The sail is blocked in its raised position, it's impossible to hoist a crew member as the halyards and blocks are now unusable. The skipper Lionel Lemonchois manages to cut *Gitana X*'s mainsail halyard by hoisting himself up using his arms. Both physically demanding and dangerous.

Alone as a great

Russell Coutts, five-times winner of the America's Cup, gives a full demonstration of how to capsize head first in San Francisco Bay. First, turn in a daring way and without factoring in the wind. Second, crash the bow. Third, tumble head first. Fourth, watch the masthead go crashing into the water, luckily without the rigging giving way. Fifth, watch the crew members holding on wherever they can. Six, wait for the boat to finally lie down and stop moving. Russell Coutts then passed through the wingsail head first after letting go. Luckily he had more of a fright than anything else.

In a fleet

(opposite) Capsizing is already risky, but in the middle of a fleet of AC45s going full speed ahead just after the start of a race, it could seriously end in tears. Jimmy Spithill damages his two bows and capsizes good and proper. Terry Hutchinson (in red) and Loïck Peyron (in black) didn't even have the time to be scared, and go past where they can.

Safety

There are always teams and boats in charge of safety during races, but those who follow catamarans normally have a bit more trouble than the rest …

Here it goes!
(left) It doesn't take much for Alain Thébault (standing on the hull) to start laughing in his legendary way, even when he has just flipped his favourite hydrofoil upside down, revealing in the process the appendages of this sailboard, which was, for a long time, the fastest in the world.

Vertical challenge
(right) These trampoline nets are not so convenient to use if you need to climb up them. The tight links are too small for feet and the material from which they are made is very aggressive on people's fingers. A sailor should definitely navigate horizontally, not vertically!

Aerial means
(top and right) Helicopter rescue missions are often the most effective in a range of up to 300 miles offshore. The shipwrecked put a dinghy in the sea and a rescue diver is lowered down to help them put on the harness, which will be used to lift them up.

Taken in tow
(above) Once on its roof, a capsized multihull is stable and can even be towed over long distances.

In any weather
(left) Sea rescues don't normally take place in the nicest of weather, as evidenced by the towing of this pleasure sailboat through strong Mistral winds by the all-weather Hyères rescue station boat close to the Island of Porquerolles.

Newport, obviously!

Nowhere on earth will you find as many beautiful, different and well-maintained boats sailed as regularly as in Newport, Rhode Island, on the north-east coast of the United States of America. Certainly Cowes, Trinité-sur-Mer, Auckland and Sydney might vie among themselves for supremacy, but none of them come anywhere near Newport. In winter, of course, everyone stays sheltered because the temperature is aggressively low, but come springtime, all manner of boats are returned to the water. Newport was home to America's most famous yacht designing/building dynasty, the Herreshoffs, it was the headquarters of the America's Cup, the base of the 12-Metre yachts, and the obligatory stopover point for maxi yachts. Everyone loves going to Newport, including those sailors who are preparing to race across the North Atlantic. Newport is also home to clam chowder and lobster, and it boasts an untold number of bars and restaurants, as well as cosy Victorian-type houses and grandiose mansions along Ocean Avenue. It is a unique and absolutely charming place.

Rhode Island
(above and top left) With Maine and Connecticut, the US state of Rhode Island is a perfect place to go for a cruise – it's where the boats are the prettiest and best maintained.

Classic sailing
(above) Sailing in Newport Bay means that you can benefit from a favourable breeze while cruising along the shoreline of immaculately kept villas and spectacular mansions. Ideal for wooden dayboats with low freeboards as they blend beautifully into the landscape.

Alternative
This is America, so you can pretty much get away with doing anything you want to, to get off the beaten track.
Why not a schooner wishbone boom rig? Close to the mansions heading for Brenton Point, this is a technique that
appears to be as effective as it is easy …

Beer time
(previous double-page spread) A beautiful summer's afternoon ends; it will soon be time to make their way back to the docks between the large yachts. From there, there should be a bar available every 10 yards or so …

Rose Island

The small Rose Island Lighthouse has seen more than one famous boat go by, and notably all the large yachts from the great era of the America's Cup, most of which were built in Narragansett Bay. The Swiss Mod 70 *Spindrift* racing towards New York keeps this tradition alive, not without giving the passing pleasure boater a small fright.

Bubbles on the ocean

Reaching
Brimming with power
thanks to their ballast
and canting keels, the
IMOCA 60 monohulls are
devilish machines when
close reaching to the shore
with reduced sail. One
wonders how the Vendée
Globe skippers can put up
with these conditions for
days on end.

Slip the mooring lines, and this time for real. As its name suggests, ocean racing has all the challenges of racing combined with the vicissitudes of the open sea.

What they never tell you is that you have to live for several weeks in the aforementioned racing boat, which means drinking, eating and sleeping in a small space that is uncomfortable, damp and shaking, with overcrowding and fractious tempers thrown in. Some prefer to go it alone, and thus create another problem, which in turn leads to several others: they have to manage everything by themselves.

In reality, an ocean-racing boat is a hermetically sealed bubble, cut off from the rest of the world, flying at full speed, and whose only aim in life is to arrive before its rivals. What might be hard to bear for one day during a regatta – being cold, wet, beaten and broken – takes on a completely different meaning when you have no other choice than to buck up and mend this moving, noisy machine you cannot leave or slow down.

Nature as a partner
The unquestionable attraction of offshore racing lies in those unique experiences in the middle of the ocean, far away from everything, battling with nature, and savouring the moment. You have only the sky and the waves as your companions, but you have all the sky: the sun rising and setting, millions of stars, clouds of every shape. And you have all the waves – small ones, nervous ones, short ones, long ones, cross swells, breaking ones, idiot waves that come out of nowhere and arrive in front of you, behind you, next to you and sometimes over you. There are also marine animals, when they feel like showing up, and other boats that always make you wonder where on earth they are coming from and where on earth they are going to? Then you hear someone say, 'Sheet in the mainsail will you, rather than contemplating the stars.' Ah yes, you

have to race throughout the night too, even at four in the morning when the need for sleep is most acute.

Undoubtedly the latest technical developments enable you to have a better quality of life on board as crew gear, communications, the precision of weather forecasts, not to mention new ways of feeding yourself and resting enable you to go better, faster and further. One thing is striking, though: the reluctance of sailors to talk about the conditions on board once they have returned to terra firma. Ocean racing seems to make you forgetful, deaf and dumb. Not that a code of silence is deliberately upheld, but the sport is occupied by men and women who are so caught up in their passion they are unaware of how extraordinary their situation is.

Monohull or multihull?
In reality, a modern racing boat is hell incarnate, managed by little devils (the sailors) who deliberately perpetuate these nightmarish conditions. There are two scenarios: the boat is either a monohull or a multihull. On a monohull, the absolute, obsessive priority is the distribution of weight – including that of the crew. You therefore have to live with the idea that everything that is not placed on the last inch of the windward side of the deck will slow the boat down. Sails, food, safety equipment, personal luggage and crew are all crammed into the same space and shifted from one side to the other with each change of tack, crew included, even these who are off duty and trying to sleep. For the ladies, who will inevitably ask what to do in case of pressing need, the answer is to use a bucket. No other provisions have been made. As to personal hygiene, wet wipes will do the job. As to food, the freeze-dried variety

Fujifilm off Ushant
This picture, taken in 2002 during the Courses des Phares never ceases to amaze due to the shape of the wave created by the opposing wind and current close to Ushant island. The trimaran ORMA 60 *Fujifilm* captained by Loïck Peyron went on to win the race hands down. The boat was destroyed a few months later in a storm during the Route du Rhum race.

is the only solution, so the kettle becomes a unique and essential piece of kit. Some connoisseurs argue that the cuisine on French boats is better than on Kiwi boats, but we will never know for sure as no one will volunteer to test this hypothesis!

On multihulls, the problem is slightly different. The little devils do not have an adrenaline pump, which means they don't feel the risks or the pressure. These sailors are not like us, mere mortals. When common sense says they should slow down, they keep their foot on the accelerator and go even faster. It doesn't matter if the weather is so foggy you can't see the bow, or if it's dark – nothing makes any difference. And do you think they slow down when it's time to rest? No way. Either they don't care and carry on steering for hours on end so as not to lose an inch, or they leave the autopilot to look after everything and go to sleep. According to their dictum: 'If you put on the brakes, you're a coward!' The visiting guest has two options: give yourself up to their expertise and just pray it will end as soon as possible, which it won't, or jump over the side and swim to shore.

From the photographic point of view, it's without doubt the most difficult subject – like trying to capture the image of ocean birds before they disappear over the other side of the horizon – but also the most spectacular, because you can take pictures in real high-sea conditions. There's no doubt that for the last ten years the speed of the sport and the media requirements of sponsors have cranked up the pressure. Nowadays there must be froth, large waves, the spectacular, the incredible – you have to feel the force of the elements facing the competitors. Because of the speed of the boats, taking pictures from a helicopter has become the norm. Obviously, because of the high cost,

this is reserved for the professionals, preferably those who work for a team, an organiser, a class or at the behest of the media, but this is becoming increasingly rare. It's the same for on-board pictures, taken sparingly because of the difficulty involved. The boat must be in the open sea under racing conditions, which is fairly unusual outside the main events. One thing is certain: no one apart from the competitors will be there at the most important time, ie, during the race itself. On the other hand, there is nothing more moving than the start of a long-distance race, notably the Vendée Globe, or more exciting than the victorious arrivals. It really is a shared joy, even if the arrival of multihulls in the dead of night surrounded by a fleet of spectator boats going at full speed can be a bit alarming! The audience becomes the spectacle.

At full speed
The maxi-trimaran *Sodebo* going full speed during a world speed record trial to cross the Mediterranean in 2012. Thomas Coville has been nearly three times around the world, racing single-handedly aboard this Irens design. A large slice of life at sea as well as a gruelling vocation.

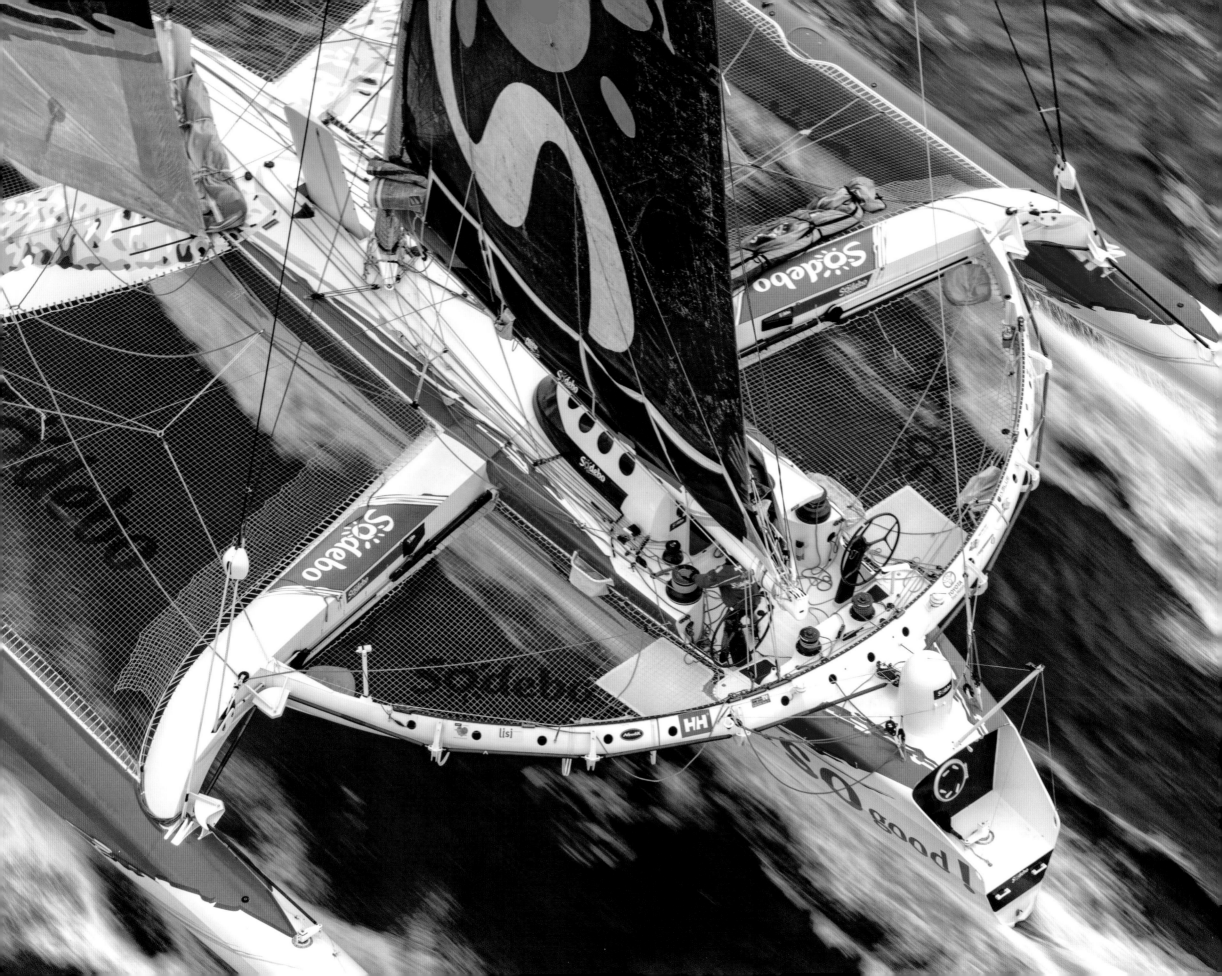

Figaro here, Figaro there
(left, top and bottom) A real melting pot in which the talents of offshore racing are born, the Figaro 2 series built by Bénéteau is original in that it often sees the most decorated skippers return to them time and again. Large doses of side by side solo racing and the same material make it a hard drug that most find difficult to kick.

Nose to the grindstone
(right) Steering for hours and hours, in the breeze and in the doldrums. This is where the millimetres, which in the end make a difference, are won. The tactical options and the correct exploitation of the weather can make or break winners, but they all have this talent that pushes them to the edge while still keeping a minimum of lucidity.

Broaching
(left) Obviously when alone in the breeze, it is not always possible to be facing the right way. Solid and forgiving, the Figaro 2 can do the most spectacular freestyle moves without flinching.

The world as a playground

The IMOCA 60 monohulls have turned the world into their playground, whether they are being sailed solo or as a pair, with a few deckchairs as bonus crew members. The Vendée Globe has become the ultimate sailing test, which fascinates crowds due to the amount of commitment it requires from the participants. Even if the first few are purely racing, there still is in their wake a gallery of high-colour portraits that tell the story of extreme lifestyles, resourcefulness, joy and hard times. Only one thing is certain: there will always be intense emotions waiting for you.

Speed machines
(left) The IMOCA 60 monohulls such as Jérémie Beyou's *Delta Dore* go by so quickly that the waves hardly have time to say hello …

The public
(top right) The emergence of an enthusiastic public at Les Sables-d'Olonne is a happy surprise that continues to grow at every Vendée Globe race. There are almost as many people cheering on the last few as the first.

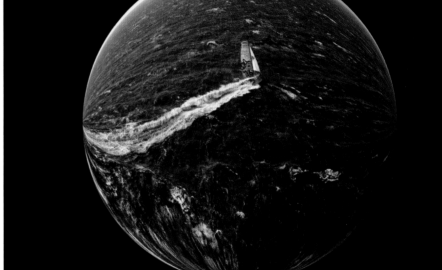

Circumnavigating
(middle right) Hellish for some, exhilarating for others, never trivial, circumnavigating the planet's seas is never an easy undertaking. To do it single-handedly and while racing is very much an extreme adventure.

Les Sables-d'Olonne
(bottom right) Going up Les Sables-d'Olonne fairway over several hundred metres through a crazed crowd is an exceptional moment that is on a par with any hype you might find at major stadium events. This is true when departing but even more so when coming back.

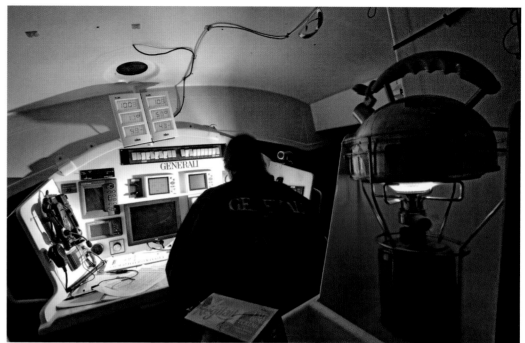

The warm glow

(left) Whether cooking freeze dried food or having a cup of tea to boost their morale, a large part of solo sailors' lives revolves around their kettle and the small blue flames of their gas cookers. A bit of life and heat in a brutal, cold and damp world.

Navigation

(top) Weather, communication, navigation, and even a little nap between manoeuvres, solo sailors spend a lot of time at the navigation station.

Sail stowage

(above) The downwind sails remain stored in the fo'c's'le if they aren't going to be useful for days on end. To get them out and rig them is a rather dynamic sport, which pushes skippers to use their full physical potential.

The cockpit
(top) Even if autopilots have come on in leaps and bounds, notably when faced with strong winds, nothing can replace the helmsman's touch in light or changeable conditions.

Bulb keel
(above) The canting keels provide extra power, but the amount of effort they induce is enormous. Several IMOCA 60 monohulls have lost their keels, but sailors sometimes manage to reach port by adjusting the water ballast to keep the boat upright.

The foredeck
(right) Even if solo sailors manage to carry out a bulk of the current manoeuvres from the cockpit, there are times when it is necessary to get soaked on the bow of the boat. One hand for yourself, one hand for the boat, and an obligatory harness to keep the two together.

Seesaw

(above) Warning, we are entering a different class, that of multihull offshore racing. Here we like to lift a hull or two, but not too much. It's mostly the adrenaline that must be managed when conditions become extreme. The rest of the time, it is simply sheer joy.

Final rush

(right) Sailing solo during the 2008 Route du Rhum race in which he would come third, Pascal Bidégorry puts his foot down to rally to the Pointe-à-Pitre finish line. A great spectacle for the local crowd, who are a bit too close for comfort!

Ocean pioneers

It is they who opened up new pathways and first left a wake along risky routes, they who pioneered new and unusual means of navigation and who broke an innumerable number of boats trying out these new ideas. Some have now passed, but all led exemplary lives chasing their dreams, and encouraging thousands of men and women to follow in their wake.

Legends of the sea
(from left to right, top to bottom) Eric Tabarly on board *Pen Duick* at Monaco Classic Week, Florence Arthaud's 1990 Route du Rhum victorious arrival, the three brothers Stéphane, Loïck and Bruno Peyron at the end of The Race in 2001, Sir Peter Blake's victorious arrival at the 1994 Jules Verne Trophy race, Olivier de Kersauson at the start of the 1997 Jules Verne Trophy, Philippe Poupon on board *Fleury Michon* (Route du Rhum, 1990), Mike Birch at the start of the 2004 Transat Jacques Vabre.

Orma 60
(right) In a multihull ORMA 60 and solo in extreme conditions, or the maritime equivalent of playing Russian roulette.

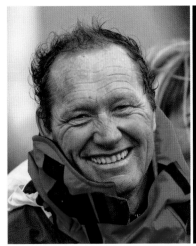

Exemplary

(previous page) *Groupama III* is the embodiment of perfect success. This is the boat that Frank Cammas wanted and captained, and with which he and his crew broke every record that came their way, notably winning the Jules Verne Trophy after two attempts. The first nearly ended badly off the New Zealand coast with a broken float, but the second went without a hitch and meant they sailed in great time to boot. This exceptional boat continues its record-breaking career under the *Banque Populaire* banner and managed by Armel Le Cléac'h.

Young sea lions

They have picked up the mantle and have upped the offshore racing stakes in terms of speed, power and distance. They have invented new records, built boats specifically to sail at incredible speeds, have fought side by side and have been there for each other for thousands of years. Engineers and builders as well as sailors, weather experts and strategists, always surrounded by competent and devoted teams, all sailors – and many others – are exemplary men and women.

The heirs

(from left to right, top to bottom) Francis Joyon, Thomas Coville, Jean Le Cam, Frank Cammas, François Gabart, Kito de Pavant, Ellen MacArthur, Michel Desjoyeaux.

Indian delights

Mauritius, the Maldives, the Seychelles, Madagascar – these are all names that cry out to be explored and excite the senses, names that are synonymous with magical archipelagos where beauty reigns supreme. It is doubtless the unlikely marriage between populations of African and Indian origin that create such a feeling of welcome and indolence here, which borders on aggression. The cruising options in this tropical paradise are not as plentiful as the Caribbean or the Mediterranean, which actually increases the feeling that you are the first to ever drop anchor here.

Needless to say, there is a lot more to see underwater than on the surface, and it would be a serious mistake not to spend as much time splashing about on the reefs as going sailing. The time difference is less punishing coming from Europe, so you can adapt more quickly and make the most of your stay. There's only one impending problem, but it's a big one: if the rise in water levels is as much as has been forecasted, the future of many of the islands will be underwater. Quick, go while there's still time!

Respect
(above) The Seychelles turtles have been here for a while, some of them can live to be nearly 200 years old. A little respect there you young 'uns please!

Maldives
(above and top left) When there is time to sweep the dead leaves that have fallen on the beach, it means that the quality of life has reached a certain higher level. And as there is no shortage of fish in the area, this can't be too far off heaven on earth.

Contrasts
Turquoise blue or golden granite, the Seychelles archipelago is only the tip of a huge sailing territory that stretches over several hundred kilometres and includes the Amirante Islands, far from everything.

Dropping anchor

(previous double-page spread) There are signs that leave no room for misinterpretation. When, instead of dropping the anchor in the water we carry the anchor to land, this can only mean two things: the first is that there is no chance of the wind turning – these are trade winds after all, and the tropics aren't far. The second is that said land is a white sandy beach, and that it is generally deserted. But, unfortunately, nothing is perfect, the rising tide will soon cover everything, there is just enough time to enjoy this paradise lost in the heart of the Maldives.

Fishing in the Maldives
The *dhoni*, the large fishing boats in the Maldives, are not very different to the dhows as depicted by Henry de Monfreid, who sailed around the Horn of Africa and the Red Sea.

Classic yachts
Revival

Eleonora
Built in 2000 as a replica of the legendary *Westward* designed and built by Nathanael Herreshoff, *Eleonora* is one of the largest classic yachts launched in the noughties. She is incredibly powerful in the breeze!

The phenomenon of restoring classic yachts is astonishing. In an age dominated by carbon fibre and sophisticated hull designs, some owners and crews prefer to delve back in history and rediscover the pleasure of sailing slowly on heavy boats with not very efficient rigs. But, oh, they are beautiful …

It was just a few minutes that changed the face of sailing. It happened during the 1991 La Nioulargue regatta in Saint-Tropez. Until then, the race created ten years earlier by Patrice de Colmont was an assortment of boats of all ages and sizes, with the IOR maxi yachts as the unrivalled stars. That year, the recently restored classic yacht *Altair* asked to join the race. She was the first schooner to be fully restored back to her original state, replicating wherever possible the original building and rigging methods. In those days most of the photographers and media people all crowded onto the same boat to follow the races, with up to 40 people on board. Some asked to have a closer look at this elegant old boat, which was beating towards Saint-Tropez. Once near, it was such a wonderful sight that there was an explosion of camera clicking. Such elegance! Such refinement, even down to the white uniforms worn by the crew, the leathered winch handles, the old fashioned-looking lines, the blocks remade in the period style, and the traditionally cut sails with their narrow panels.

Then the cameras and people gradually fell silent. The sight of this boat under sail was so magnificent and so dazzling that everyone just wanted to savour the moment, to contemplate it in silence, just for the pleasure of looking and of appreciating the thousand and one details of this purist restoration. It was a magical moment and nothing else on the water mattered, until *Altair* crossed the finish line and lowered her sails. Classic yachts and the restoration movement had arrived.

A real international circuit

Ever since, every season sees a new batch of big and small boat restorations, from simple traditional craft to J-Class yachts and much more besides. Not just old boats found pickled in their juices and restored at vast expense, but also replicas built from scratch, such as the enormous three-masted schooner *Atlantic*. Owners have greeted this new form of sailing with enthusiasm, and a vibrant international race circuit has emerged. For it didn't take long for races to be organised for the old boats, some of them losing their rigs or the integrity of their hulls in the process, before skippers learned not to push these old relics as hard as their carbon fibre counterparts. They need room to breathe, gentle movements, building up speed rather than pointing too high into the wind, and not attacking the start line as you would do with a dinghy. It is a question of caution, anticipation and avoiding at all costs situations that might lead to a collision.

Launched in the Mediterranean, the phenomenon spread around the world. Simultaneously, the interest in seafaring heritage stretched to working boats, and then big square-riggers, whose appearances in Tall Ships' races attract thousands of spectators. French sailing legend Eric Tabarly got his family yacht *Pen Duick* back on the water, and key figures such as Elizabeth Meyer applied themselves to the restoration of the J-Class. The reappearance of Meyer's *Endeavour* marked a turning point. Since then, the J-Class has become as active as in its heyday of the 1930s, with both restored old boats and sublime modern replicas racing together.

The remarkable thing, however, is that, despite the large number of restorations, some boats always stand out, even after changing owner or captain, as if the yacht's elegance, charm, style and sailing ability were inbred. This is the case with *Altair*, which remains an inexhaustible source of beautiful pictures year after year, and *Moonbeam of Fife III*,

Estérel Massif
A classic tack no matter how you look at it, which brings sailors back to race from the buoy placed at the foot of the mountainous Estérel towards the gulf during Les Voiles de Saint-Tropez.

Moonbeam IV, *Mariquita*, as well as smaller yachts such as the 15-Metre *Tuiga*, the flagship of the Monaco Yacht Club, and *Avel*, whose elegant crew has always done justice to the Gucci family, who maintain her along with the imposing three-masted black-hulled Creole.

Aesthetics and fairness

All these boats and many more create a remarkable spectacle, both in harbour and at sea, and create magic moments that live on in the public's memory. And, as luck would have it, it's often at Les Voiles de Saint-Tropez that this takes place. One year it will be the enormous *Adix* flattened by a gust of wind, another year it will be the first nail-biting meeting between two old J-Class yachts, or the tack-by-tack contest between *Atlantic* and *Creole*, or the crazy pedal to the metal surfing of the unstable *Bona Fide*.

These are brief moments when several boats of great style line up and put on a spectacular show, wonderful to watch because of the beauty of the yachts and the technical skills of their crew. Sometimes it's just the sound of bagpipes or of a violin emerging from one of the boats as they leave their moorings and head for the start line, or a perfect line-up of 12-Metre yachts sailing at full pelt, or the return of a whole fleet of classic yachts in front of the Estérel mountains, glowing red in the autumnal afternoon light. You have to be ready to see everything, to hear everything. The moment will come. For sure.

From the photographic point of view, it's pure joy! The boats are beautiful, the crews well dressed, there is no aggressive advertising on the sails or the hulls, and they move slowly so you can follow them without too much difficulty. And, if the wind happens to be strong, the show will be all the more impressive, because there is no finer sight than heavy boats, low on the water, pitching and rolling and crashing through the waves. Add to this a certain way of life, parties once the boats are back in harbour, hardware, rigging, varnish and teak decks that make perfect still lifes, and you'll see why classic yachts are so popular among amateur photographers, who can be sure of producing beautiful images.

Hailstones
To sail on an old boat means to sail in all weather, including knowing how to deal with a gust of hail in the middle of the Bay of Cannes during a particularly trying 2006 edition of the Régates Royales.

Mariska
(right) 15-Metre yachts are among the most elegant boats ever built. The restoration of one of them, here *Mariska*, designed by William Fife III in 1908, proves that it is well worth starting more or less from scratch to see the boat sail once more.

Alcyon
(left) The reconstructed *Alcyon* revisits the Fort Saint-Jean In Marseille, where it used to sail more than a century ago with numerous identical boats racing in the Mediterranean. She might have a waterline length of less than 23ft (7m), but she makes up for it with the exaggerated size of her sailplan.

Square

(opposite page) Welcome on board *Altair*, the legendary schooner designed for cruising by William Fife III in 1937. Her restoration in 1987 by Fairlie Restoration has set the gold standard for the restoration of classic yachts.

Appearance

(above) In order to accommodate the aesthetic taste of classic yacht owners, the manufacturers of deck fittings have developed a range of specific equipment such as winches with bronze drums.

Etiquette

(above) Maritime tradition requires that you have the ability to communicate with flags, and it is always best to keep the 26 letters organised alphabetically. Speaking of which, isn't that what the Chinese do?

It's all in the detail

Classic yachts are beautiful, and their interior design even more so. In this case, it's all in the detail, whether it's the respect for building techniques or the comfort levels and décor of the time. Space is usually limited as the hulls are narrow, and light is rare and subdued through the small portholes. Without forgetting that when sailing, all this antique furniture has a tendency to lean rather a lot!

Structure

(above) The interior of *Elsinore*, an 8mR designed and built by Tore Holm in 1930.

Magic
(left) Only classic sailing is able to create exceptional moments such as this alignment of *Eleonora*, *Mariette*, *Sunshine*, *Moonbeam IV* and *Moonbeam of Fife III* off the coast of Monaco during the 15-Metre *Tuiga*'s centennial celebrations in 2009.

Pen Duick
(right) Five yachts have the same name and all share the same legendary founding father Eric Tabarly. They still sail and adore to tack together. From left to right: the schooner *Pen Duick III*, the gaff cutter *Pen Duick*, the large ketch *Pen Duick VI*, the yawl *Pen Duick II* and the little ballast sloop *Pen Duick V*.

Trilogy
Some yachts such as *Altair* (left), *Moonbeam of Fife III* (right, top and bottom) and *Lelantina* (middle right) are the pillars of classic yacht circuits and know how to hold their rank. During the 2013 Les Voiles de Saint-Tropez, these three tough guys went out with 20–30 knots of wind and rough seas when their peers preferred to stay in port. A nice maritime gesture.

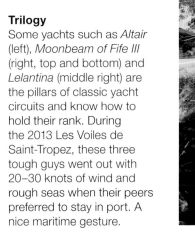

Blow out
(right) 'What do we do now?' A spinnaker is ripped by a gust of wind that blew a little bit too quickly, and the crew of *Eilean*, a cutter designed by Fife III and launched in 1936, now have a problem on their hands. There's going to have to be a lot of hands on deck to retrieve the damaged material.

Butterfly effect
(above) Rigging overexposure on Vele d'Epoca di Imperia 2006 swell between the small gaff rigged *Lona II* and the huge 19-Metre cutter *Mariquita*, which is, however, not much faster in these light winds.

Hoist up high
(above) Everything is done through muscle power on board *Mariquita*. The hoisting of the huge gaff mainsail requires all hands on deck, and the crew find their rhythm using a traditional maritime song. Beautiful.

La Belle Classe

Created in 2005 by the Monaco Yacht Club, which has always supported classic yachts, La Belle Classe only accepts exceptionally restored or rebuilt boats in accordance with best standard practices. They also stand for fair play, elegance, *savoir-vivre*, maritime heritage, quality service and respect for the environment.

Mariette
(left) The large schooner *Mariette* has had a sometimes shaky career with, notably, its involvement in the 1995 fatal accident that saw the demise of La Nioulargue, which has since become Les Voiles de Saint-Tropez. The boat remains superb and her rigging requires the vertical intervention of one of her crew members to help set the topsails and mizzen staysail.

Atlantic
(right) We owe quite a few great yacht renaissances to the skipper Ed Kastelein, but the construction project of a replica of the *Atlantic* will no doubt remain his masterpiece. Charlie Barr's three-masted schooner can once more be admired by generations of sailors to come.

Risky business
Classic boat crews
sometimes take some
serious risks to gain a
few places when going
around the buoys or when
they have to manoeuvre
in the breeze. To their
credit, old yachts do
not have unparalleled
manoeuvrability, and
handling the sails, often
with limited equipment,
calls for a solid knowledge
of maritime tradition,
a lot of sailing sense
and a strong dose of
inventiveness.

The Pacific, the north side

It's not an obvious cruising destination, but somewhere you sail to for the simple reason that many people live there, and yet it's out of range of most boatowners. San Diego Bay in southern California is the landmark favoured by many famous sailors, chief among them Dennis Conner, and it is the ideal base for those planning a cruise in the Sea of Cortez. San Francisco Bay and the Golden Gate have enough seafaring history to warrant a pilgrimage in themselves, following in the footsteps of Jack London.

Recent America's Cup adventures have revealed a talent for staging a memorable sailing spectacle, even if the sea and air are chilly and the fog quite persistent in the middle of summer. Further north towards Seattle and British Columbia, against a backdrop of rocky mountains, there's a maze of canals packed with wildlife, which is a haven for nature lovers. The currents are strong, the sun doesn't shine every day, but this only adds a layer of authenticity to the seafaring life. It's a marvellous playground.

Chilly sailing
Whether in San Diego Bay (top) or sailing on British Columbian waters (above), the north Pacific waters remain cold throughout the year and force local sailing enthusiasts to wrap up warm as soon as there is a light breeze.

Orcas
As well as the majestic landscapes, another main attraction in British Columbia is the abundance of marine life, which is as varied in size as in shape. Orca pods are regularly seen in these parts.

Golden Gate Bridge
Sailing under the Golden Gate Bridge, the entrance to San Francisco Bay, remains the dream of all sailors bitten by the travel bug. Choose your day wisely though as there is a high probability you won't see a thing due to the heavy fog that normally reigns in this place, especially at the start of summer.

San Diego Bay
(previous double-page spread) Back to the training ground for the trimaran *USA 17* in San Diego Bay. The South Californian climate is definitely one of the most pleasant in the world, even if the drought causes some serious problems.

The enclosed bay usually has light winds and should lead to worry-free sailing. You just have to remember to give priority to aircraft carriers crossing, as San Diego is also the main USA west coast military port.

Mount Baker
Typical British Columbian landscape. Winding channels interlaced with strong currents, grandiose decor with a mountainous rocky backdrop within reach, with Mount Baker (3,286m) reigning over the land.

The America's Cup

An old lady on top form!

Adrenaline
High-speed street fighting with the Golden Gate Bridge in the background. The America's Cup, the world's oldest sporting trophy, has transformed itself by adopting the most extreme machines imaginable: multihulls on foils propelled by immense rigid wing sails.

The wonders of the America's Cup! There's nothing quite like it for manufacturing dreams and illusions. Few contests can generate so many misconceptions, heated debates and falsehoods, so much excitement or abject hatred, and, above all, such resounding technical and sporting achievements.

Following ten editions of this race over 30 years gives you the opportunity to question a few key ideas that are sometimes forgotten in the heat of the moment but which form the mainstay of this event unlike any other.

Firstly, the America's Cup is absolutely not the highest pinnacle of a sport hierarchy operated by an international federation. Quite the opposite. It is a completely private contest that has nothing to do with the international sailing government bodies and whose only driving force are the personal dreams of victory of those who hope to win it.

The main players are either wealthy individuals who have set their hearts on participating in the most exclusive hobby in the world, or sailors of international renown who want to make it the highest point of their career or, more prosaically, others who just want a job to keep them going for another few years. The challenge for the first is to surround themselves with trustworthy people and produce the alchemy that will lead to eventual victory. The challenge for the second is to amass a colossal sum of money very quickly to get started in good time and have the best chance of clinching the prize. None of this prevents them dressing the whole thing up in a cloak of nationalism, the better to tempt sponsors, companies, official bodies and even the public at large into helping and supporting them. All things considered, however, it all boils down to ego.

Every time, it's just a few decision-makers from each team who play the high stakes of the America's Cup, a kind of highly cerebral game of chess that involves several disciplines: finance, human relations, risk assessment, organisation, logistics, external relations, communication, planning and operation management. Naval architecture? Technology?

Yes, of course, but success will depend who is chosen and their ability to work together. Sailing? Sport? Yes, there will have to be a bit of those in the end, but they are just the tiny, visible tip of the iceberg. And they are only the result of everything that has gone before. There is one rule in this strange old world that suffers no exception: 'The America's Cup is always won long before the final race. You only race to find out by whom.'

The trophy and the act

The second intangible element is this: the America's Cup is made up of two inseparable things, one of which is known by everyone and the other of which is never seen. Everyone knows this trophy of questionable aesthetic value, which is so public it has to be protected by bodyguards, but only a few have seen the piece of paper that should always accompany it: the Deed of Gift. And the most important of the two is not the one you'd think. The Deed of Gift sets out the rules of the America's Cup and is so set in stone that only the President of the United States of America could modify it following a legal process that would be so long and hazardous that no one has ever dared try it – even though successive holders of the 'Auld Mug' have desperately wanted to!

The man who created the deed when he donated the trophy to the New York Yacht Club, George L Schuyler, was co-owner of the schooner *America*, the winner of the inaugural race at Cowes in 1851. He produced a document of exemplary clarity, which stipulated that the trophy holder – the last winner of the title – was obliged to put it back in play when challenged by anyone through a yacht club. Having spent a fortune winning the Cup, the winner therefore has only one obligation:

The trophy
The America's Cup trophy with, in the background, the replica of the schooner that won what was then the 100 Guinea Cup in August 1851 at Cowes. Only the top section of the ewer existed back then. Two successive bases have been added since to accommodate the names of the winners, which are systematically etched after every race.

to put their hand in their pocket and mount a defence. In this way, the NYYC had to politely respond to 24 challenges – all of which it won – before the 'Auld Mug' was finally snatched by the Australians in 1983. The Deed of Gift gives the two sides equal say in deciding the race rules (type of boat, location, course, regulations), but imposes minimal rules itself to avoid misinterpretation.

The law of the Defender

Because the third element certainly is this: it is a totally unfair game, which is where the problems start. Masquerading under a certain impartiality, the regulations give the Defender a lot of leeway to make up their own rules. The main thing is not to go too far and get caught out, as happened with *Alinghi* at the start of the 33rd edition. The yacht club with which the Société Nautique de Genève agreed the rules of the 33rd race was a puppet outfit. That's all it took for Larry Ellison to jump into the breach and reduce the proposed race protocol to pulp.

The Defender is always regarded with suspicion. The history of the Cup is littered with these little arrangements, which make the challengers howl in protest but leave the more experienced unmoved: 'To complain about the Defender is like complaining about your mother-in-law. If you don't like it, then go and play somewhere else.'

The truth, as always, is rarely what it seems. Welcome to the kingdom of hypocrisy, subterfuge, pretence, propaganda, phoney announcements, wild rumour, very private secret negotiations (in other words, eventually espionage), but also illusions conjured by the very best masters of the art – and the press is often the first to fall for it all. Politics reign supreme in the America's Cup, and it is best to wait and see the truth with your own eyes or to read the official notifications to avoid a lot of useless speculation.

Finally, it's nearly always the fastest boat that wins. Even if the team takes a week of racing and is reduced to a score of 1-8 before finding its wings, the incredible return of James Spithill and his men at San Francisco in 2013 proves, if proof were needed, that it is easier to win regattas with a faster boat, and that in spite of this dictum, the America's Cup deserves its title of queen of all races.

From the photographic point of view, the America's Cup is an infinitely rich subject. There are the crews, the boats, the training sessions on the water, the races, the VIPs, the physical training sessions on land, the crews' uniforms, the designers, the research, the media, the public both on land and at sea, the host city, the press conferences, the crew's working lives, their day-to-day activities … But there are also the ancillary events such as concerts, the land-based activities organised for the public, especially for children, the parties, and of course the America's Cup – the trophy itself. The only problem is that it lasts a long time, and part of the action is sometimes well hidden beneath opaque barriers (security borders on the paranoid at team bases), and competition is fierce because there is worldwide interest. Not to mention the key moment when the winner raises the trophy above their head. That's when your equipment needs to be very ready and you need to be prepared to shoot like a machine gun, as it is those pictures and no others that stand a chance of surviving in the long history of the America's Cup.

Alinghi
Raised by a wave during the 2007 race in Valencia, the winner's bow looks monstrous. The team, created by the Swiss Ernesto Bertarelli, dominated the America's Cup from 2003 to 2007 and, in Valencia, organised one of the races that will go down in history as being an immense success. A little bit too greedy during the next instalment, *Alinghi* was finally beaten on multihulls in 2010 after two years of trials.

Carte blanche

Rarely has a situation been as straightforward (from a technical point of view) than it was for the 33rd America's Cup race. Everything was allowed on the technical front apart from a waterline length, which was limited to 90ft (27m). Pure research ensued: towing tank (top left), aerodynamic tunnel, architecture, sophisticated construction (right, top and bottom), materials, and even empirical wing lift testing (bottom left). The *Alinghi* and *Oracle* architectural teams really enjoyed themselves.

Gigantic

(left) You had to have the entrepreneurial spirit of Larry Ellison, CEO of the software firm Oracle, to dare to launch the construction of the largest rigid wing for a boat ever built. And by a long shot. A real monster that nobody in the BMW Oracle Racing team was ever really sure would work ...

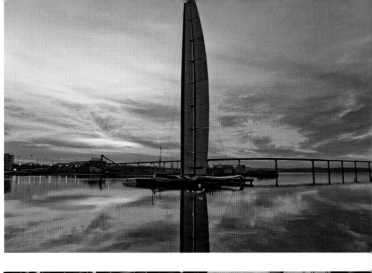

Mythical
The rigid wing trimaran
USA 17 and the catamaran
Alinghi will go down in
the already very colourful
America's Cup history
as two of the most
extreme boats ever built.
Great wind machines
and a source of endless
surprising images!

Collision course
One of the few points agreed on by two rivals of the AC33 was that there should be a very long start line to avoid being side by side. This didn't stop Jimmy Spithill, *USA 17*'s skipper, from rushing forward with his float mid-air right from the start of the race. *Alinghi* still managed to have a better start but was then overtaken by sheer speed during the first and only upwind leg.

Winners

(left) By winning for the first time the America's Cup after two years of legal battles and the construction of one of the most daring boats of all time, Larry Ellison brings the old silver pitcher back to the United States. He gives rigid wing multihulls a place in the America's Cup. Photos left to right: James Spithill, Russell Coutts, Larry Ellison, John Kostecki.

Domination

(above) Things were clear from the outset of the second race of the 33rd America's Cup in Valencia. The USA 17 displayed superior speeds both upwind and downwind. This race is the minimum planned race course in the Deed of Gift, a simple upwind-downwind 20 miles per leg.

Airborne

(following double-page spread) The USA 17 in action. Unfortunately, she will never sail again. A real shame. Like a number of extraordinary boats created for the America's Cup, including the legendary Reliance, this machine is as fragile as she is spectacular and difficult to get in working order.

AC34

The 34th America's Cup changed everything: shorter and more dynamic routes in San Francisco Bay that were close to land, boats became hydrofoil catamarans, media coverage that included live broadcasts and particular consideration given to the general public, who were treated to a series of concerts in the America's Cup Park. The participating teams had to learn to handle the huge wings twice a day and sailors had to learn how to look after their physical shape even more so than before.

Coaching

(above) Between the endless coffee-grinding sessions to get the on-board hydraulic pressure up and the telling-offs from the boss Patrizio Bertelli, the Italian team's days were pretty full during the 2013 Louis Vuitton Cup, in which they came second.

The look

(left and top) In their astronaut's outfits, the *Luna Rossa* crew win the prize for the most innovative look, which is not surprising given their sponsor's activity – as unique as it is impressive. Apart from their protective qualities, the helmets also serve to protect the indispensable communication systems.

Full speed ahead

(right) The Swedish *Artemis* team suffered the worst imaginable situation with Andrew Simpson's fatal accident just before the start of the 2013 Louis Vuitton Cup. They still managed to meet the challenge of constructing a second boat, which only partook in a handful of races before being eliminated.

Invincible

(left) The *Emirates Team New Zealand* appeared during the elimination phase of the 2013 Louis Vuitton Cup, during which they dominated from the top of their foils. The New Zealand team set the pace right up to the final race. First to sail, first to 'foil', first to put a second boat on the water, the Kiwis got (nearly) everything right in their preparations …

Louis Vuitton Cup

(top right) 'To win the America's Cup one first has to win the Louis Vuitton Cup', an event that determines which challenger will be allowed to meet the defender. Dean Barker succeeded in this first step twice, in 2007 and 2013, but was unable to clinch the final (or Cup) on either occasion. Should we change the saying?

Dalt

(middle right) The man passing from one side of *ETNZ* to the other is Grant Dalton, the fearless *Team New Zealand* boss who took over in 2003. He carefully avoids walking on the fairing (which improves the airflow below the wing). At 57, he promised he would stop sailing at the next race. Should we believe him?

Exhaustion

(bottom right) AC72 crews often become exhausted due to endless coffee-grinding sessions interlaced with sprints on the trampoline to get from one side to the other.

On the limits

Emirates Team New Zealand came extremely close to becoming the first boat to capsize during an America's Cup race. The Kiwis had done all their preparation work, but unfortunately the pressure felt during a race cannot be replicated during training …

Nosedive

(right) Going in head first. How to give yourself a good scare without causing too much damage during the first official 2013 Louis Vuitton Cup race. Two men fell overboard and were rescued immediately by chase boats. Quite an impressive way to apply the brakes, wouldn't you say?

Defender
(above and right) 'Two boats from the same team racing is a bit like dancing with your own sister.' Although they managed to master the logistics that are involved in launching two AC72s on a daily basis, the *Oracle Team USA* didn't manage to reach their full potential on the first day of the race against *Team New Zealand*. *Oracle Team USA*'s fantastic management of the final and the progress they made during the race allowed them to win it (just).

Frisco
(left) The traditional monohull circling during the phases that precede the start of the race has been replaced by a meeting at full speed between the two opponents just before they cross the starting line. Quicker but still spectacular, especially in reduced visibility conditions.

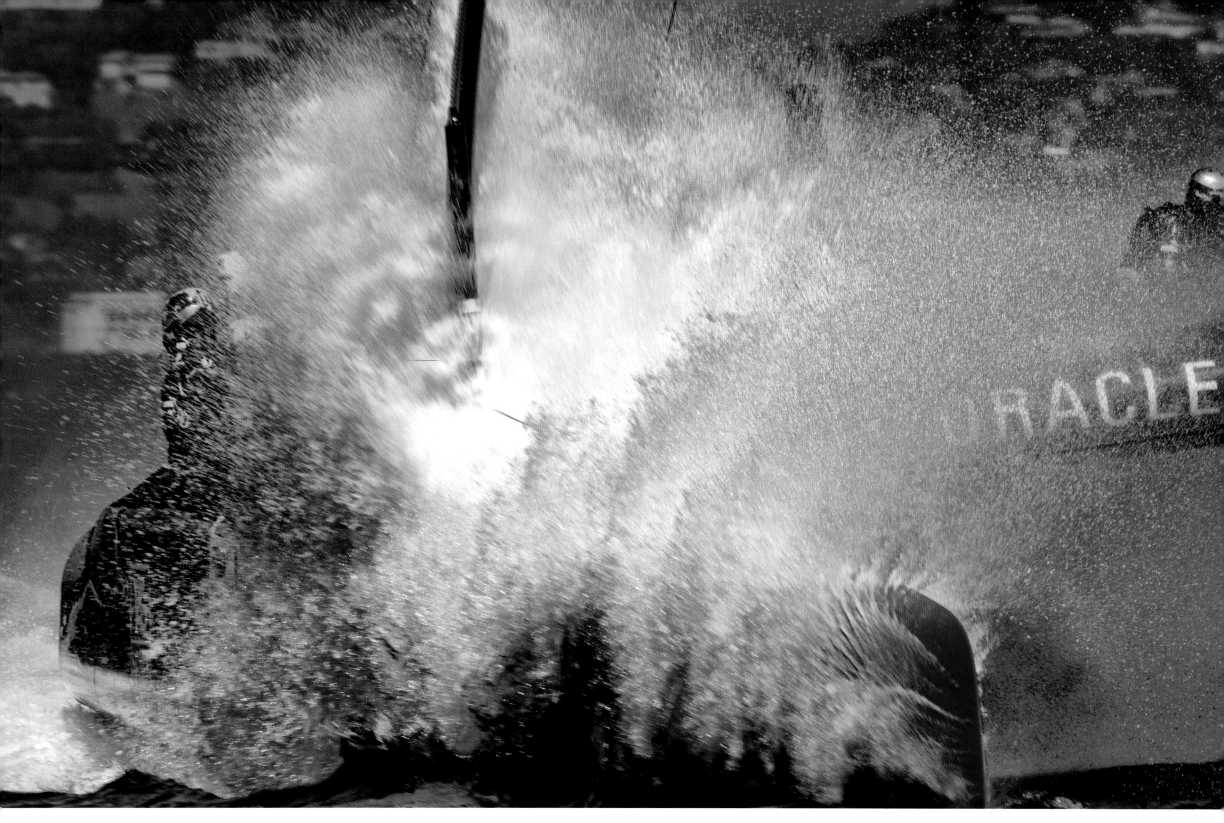

Wipeout
So long as an AC72 sails on its foils, it goes very quickly and with apparent ease. But wait. Things get more complicated when the wind dies down, there is a delay in some adjustment or a technical problem that forces a rather powerful 'wipeout'…

And breathe
The same situation from a bird's-eye view, this time on the New Zealand side. During a couple of very long seconds, the helmsman can't see a thing in front of him. As his boat is travelling at over 30 knots, that's a lot of distance covered blindly, very quickly …

Jimmy

(top left) James Spithill is an enthusiastic fellow who grabs life with both hands without asking too many questions. His ability and determination allowed the USA team to come back from a hopeless 8–1 score.

Team USA

(middle left) The final result of the 34th America's Cup is all the more surprising due to the *Oracle Team USA* going through the psychological stage of feeling 'beaten' when *Team New Zealand* was leading by a mile in what should have been the last race, but which they ended outside of the time limit.

Larry

(bottom left) Larry Ellison doesn't smile in public, not even as he lifts the America's Cup above his head. Deep down what he loves more than anything is to win, and sailing suits him down to the ground (or water!).

Craziness

Pushed to the outside of the turn on the very last race, James Spithill dares to do something crazy: make his boat dive for a fraction of a second to slow it down and gybe first. It is as though he has slammed the brakes on while going straight ahead!

The timeless charm of Polynesia

Everything is better here. Right in the middle of the oceanic world, far away from any continents, between the stars and the sea. The South Pacific draws its strength from its cosmic presence. It is so vast, so far away from everything, so entrenched in the sea that it is closer to the universe than it is to the rest of planet Earth. There's as much happening below the water as above, in terms of animal life and currents, and the protruding islands are merely the outpouring of the immense chaos churning in its depths. The paradise above is the result of the hell below. But what paradise! It's hard to understand how anyone could deny that Bora Bora and its lagoon is one of the most beautiful anchorages on Earth. Some say it's too accessible, too busy, too well known, too overrated. No, no, no and no again – it's just perfect!

Pleasure

(above and top left) French Polynesia offers many magical moments, from tacking on a Hobie Cat across the Bora Bora lagoon to climbing up the heights of Raiatea to see its red steeple against the turquoise lagoon.

Pals

(above) There's many more pals under the water than above it when you are in the middle of the Pacific Ocean, and men and women have learned to live with the inhabitants of this underwater world.

The office
Silence, men at work! Apart from the background sound of the surf on the reef and the calling of a few birds, there aren't many around to disturb the calm surroundings of this pearl farm hut. In the background is Bora Bora.

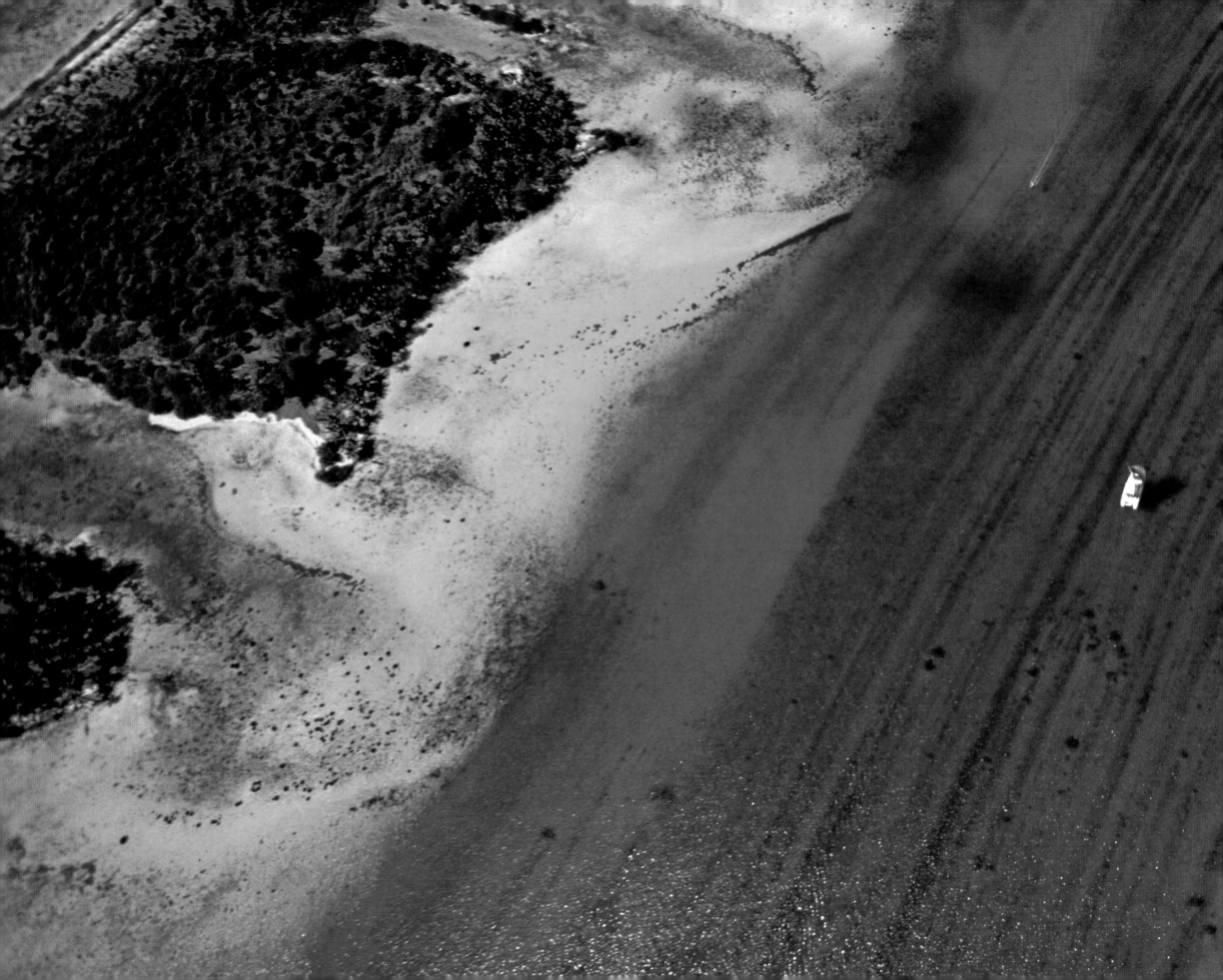

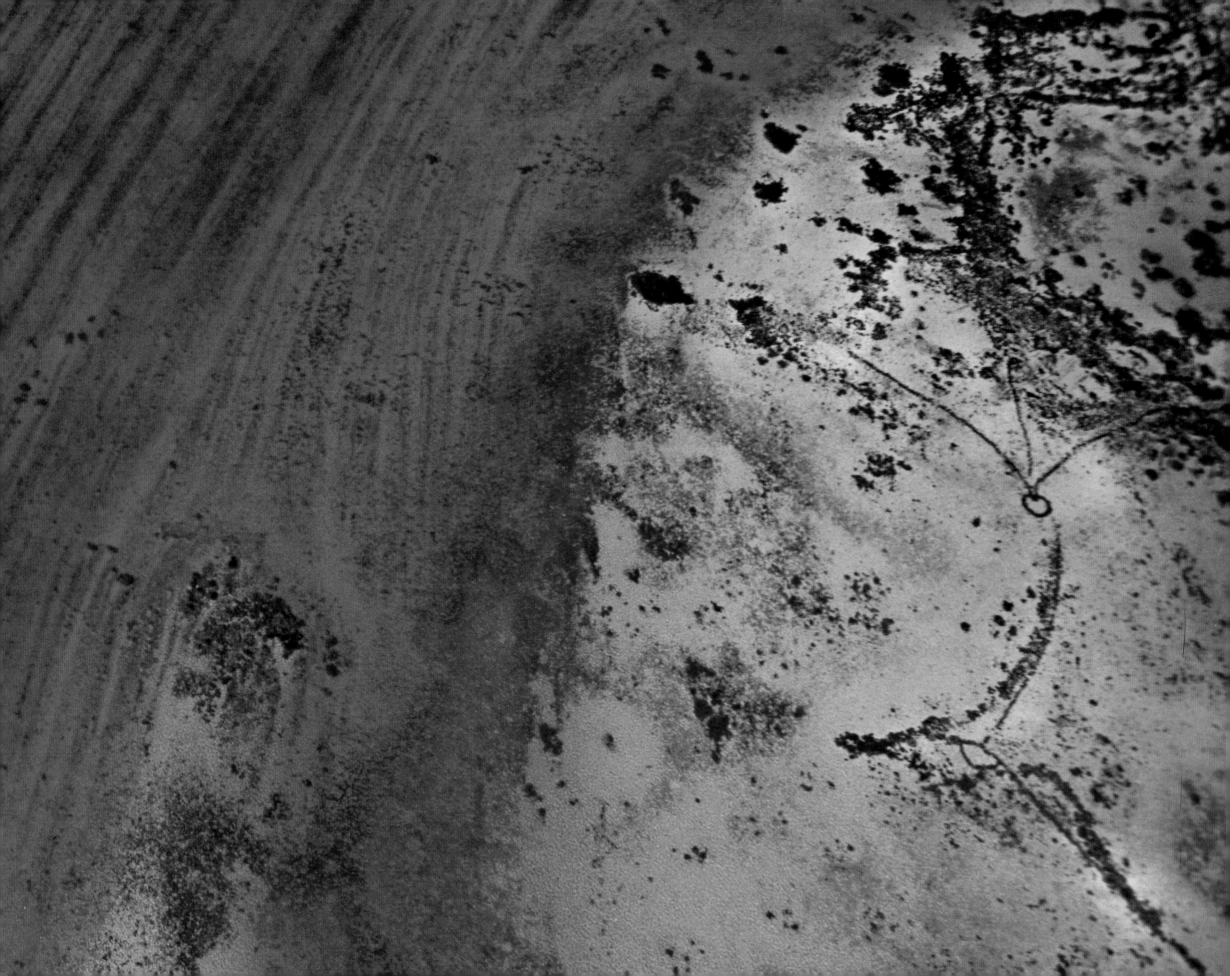

The motorway
(previous double-page spread) No need to consult your GPS to sail in the Polynesian lagoons, all you have to do is follow the colours. Navy blue, no problem getting passed; turquoise blue, the level is going up; dark brown, there's going to be some friction! Just avoid sailing facing the sun …

What else?
A surfboard, maybe? A Laser? A Hobie Cat? Or just a small outrigger to draw some tacks across this exquisite breeze? Or else nothing more, just a bit of a splash around while not doing much. Or should I say, absolutely nothing!

Cruising
The next anchorage

Sunset
Sailing is also the art of tacking just for the joy of it. Granted, we can't always do as we please to the forces of nature, waves, the wind and the tides, but for the rest, we choose our route, our destination, our timings, our equipment and even our mooring neighbours. A space in which to feel truly free.

Racing is great, but cruising is better! Especially on a modern yacht built for you to enjoy the journey and the company of your fellow travellers, rather than spending all your time honing your sailing skills in the boat.

Sailing is, in the final analysis, a pure dream. Setting off towards distant shores, pushed by the wind towards deserted islands where crystal-clear waters form enchanted anchorages … What a pleasure it is to get away from the chatter of modern life, far away from cities, cars, advertising, 24/7 news, dreadful pollution. On board, you can live close to nature, you can choose whatever route takes your fancy, you can steer a little to the left or right without any dire consequence and, if perchance the wind requires you to adjust your course, well, it can wait until you finish your cup of tea.

This is a time for reading, conversation, doing nothing, and planning nothing more than the next anchorage. And the next anchorage is important. It's what fuels the dream. You imagine it deserted, well sheltered, surrounded by glorious countryside, with clear, beautifully coloured water, good holding ground for the anchor, with a little beach not far away, and a picturesque restaurant in which to spend the evening. It shouldn't be too far away, just far enough so you can hoist your sails and drift for a few hours and enjoy sailing without a timetable. After all, what else is a successful cruising trip if not just a long succession of 'next anchorages'?

A house, a cabin, a hut …

Yes, it certainly seems so. Just one question, then: why does a skipper always get back from cruising exhausted and dreaming of going on holiday – this time for real – in the middle of nowhere, in a quiet house in the middle of the countryside? A house that doesn't move, which has all the space you need, where the children can play without worrying the grown-ups, where they can't break anything, can't drop anything overboard, and there isn't anything for them to get hurt on. A shed that won't be attacked by the neighbours in the middle of the night as soon as the wind changes direction, which isn't vulnerable to summer storms, where water and electricity are available in abundance so you won't have to nag people who take endless showers. A shack, even, with a meadow in front where the dog or cat can do their business on their own; where guards don't wake you up in the early hours to collect mooring fees. A house far away from everyone, where you won't have to endure loud and tipsy neighbours crashing their way home in the middle of the night and playing outdated disco music until dawn. A pretty, hassle-free hole where you can sleep at night, rather than continually asking yourself if your anchor is going to hold as the wind blows stronger. And, while we're on the subject, why does the wind always blow stronger at night?

A nice little dump with solid foundations, where you don't have to worry about whether your course leads to an invisible rock and which won't be buffeted by unforeseen currents. A small, unpretentious house, where you don't give a damn about the fog and the rain because the roof really is waterproof, and where you won't forget to shut the windows when it rains. A hut where you don't have to keep a toolbox close to hand, a hand-bearing compass around your neck, one eye on the GPS, another on the depth sounder. A simple refuge, where the toilets don't get blocked, the fridge makes real ice cubes, and which has an arbour where you can shelter from the sun for the first few days. A house that is so much cheaper, because you use it more than two weeks a year, you don't have to worry if there's any space left in the harbour, you know it won't get damaged in the winter storms, it doesn't need to be slipped

Porquerolles
Take the small Porquerolles pass, leave the Jeaune Garde Lighthouse and the small Langoustier fort to starboard, hear the cicadas singing in the pine forests and look through the mooring map to find the one where we will stop. Get your programme here!

or painted with antifouling, and you don't need to spend a fortune on refitting it every spring before you can use it.

Out of this world

Oh yes, a house with no engine to break down, which you don't have to constantly fill up with fuel, always spilling some on the deck; a well-built house with modern plumbing and gravity drainage that doesn't need any kind of pump or stuffing box. A house that doesn't need a bloody dinghy, which you don't know what to do with, and which you have to lower and raise, and lower and raise again, all day long.

A stress-free holiday home without cares for its captain who can SLEEP at last and take a nap without worrying about whether the medium-range weather forecast means you will have to lift the anchor and head back sooner than planned. So you're not stuck in a port somewhere, while the rest of the crew head home at the end of the school holidays and leave you there on your own. A holiday home that means its owner doesn't come back from sailing cross-eyed, while the rest of the family cry out: 'Really? I thought this year's cruise was wonderful. Thank you, my darling!' Yeah, right…

From the photographic point of view, there's nothing worse than trying to sum up a cruising holiday in pictures! Why saddle yourself with all this equipment and force yourself to take pictures when you could enjoy the moment? You never want to be on the other side of the lens more than now. You have to get up early, crawl through the grass to photograph your lovely anchorage from afar, stay in the dinghy while everyone else is swimming, always tidy down below rather than letting things go a little, organise the sailing, the anchorages, keep changing

location even though you'd rather stay in each one for an eternity. But of course, you might have to do this in the Caribbean in the middle of winter, or in southern Corsica in spring, or in any number of places most people only dream of and will probably never see. So you have to make the most of it.

Bréhat or Lavezzi?
When sailing, take the time to play between the rocks, whether close to Île de Bréhat, in northern Brittany, or under the Lavezzi Lighthouse in south Corsica. The two look so alike …

Tweaking
(right) Standard sailing boats' sails aren't always very exciting, but if you are lucky enough to benefit from a nice set of sails, then adjusting them becomes a pleasant hobby.

Manoeuvring
(above) Bright spinnaker socks, battened mainsails, automatic reefing points and jib rollers. Progress resulting from racing has made life a lot easier for the regular boaters.

Sharing
(left) Whether with friends or family, more than anything sailing gives people the chance of having some quality time with loved ones and friends. It's a shame for those who prefer to sail solo, but they seem to have a great time too!

Sailing
(right) Modern cruising yachts don't let you down in terms of performance. Well, most don't. It's mostly their average size that has increased, both in real terms and in what is perceived as a 'large' boat, a term now devoted to boats over 53ft (16m) long.

Pulpit

(left) While cruising, you can do what even the best racers in the world aren't ever allowed to, like, for example, daydreaming on the little bench located at the end of the bow …

Bathing platform

(above) One of the best inventions for modern cruising sailboats remains the bathing platform, which allows you to enjoy the sea more when it beckons to be swum in, and also aids the loading and unloading of on board games …

Victualling

(above) A lot of time is spent preparing, consuming and tidying while cruising, but also discussing reprovisioning and the next meals. No doubt because space is limited but also because you finally have the time to take an interest in basic elements relating to our existence.

Gargalo

(right) Two metres (6ft 6in) below the keel, 2m on each side, there isn't much more room in the passage that separates the island of Gargalo to the rest of Corsica in the heart of the nature reserve on the Scandola peninsula. To be visited in fine weather only.

Tenders

(above) Small, big, inflatable or hard, motorised or with oars, the dinghy is vital on a cruising boat as it gives people the ability to escape when the boat is moored.

Young 'uns
There are plenty of places where children could hurt themselves on a boat, but also lots of places to have fun and games. It's a question of balance and supervision. Clearly, for this, catamarans are both more spacious and safer.

Starry night

(below) Even at night, sailing can cause both young and old to be amazed; the absence of light pollution makes for some wonderful stargazing.

Plugged in

(right) Much like racing boats, cruising boat navigation stations have evolved more towards electronic equipment. Paper charts haven't completely disappeared yet, but how long before they do?

On autopilot

(right) Gone are the endless hours of sailing at the helm, especially during motorised delivery trips. Long live autopilots and GPS locators. And the course won't change an iota should the helmsman decide to relax a little …

Isolation

(opposite page) The other big advantage of cruising catamarans is the possibility of isolating yourself. The cabins are better separated, and even on deck one can always find a little peaceful corner of paradise, if needed.

Lazing around
Let us plunge into the crystal waters of a Mediterranean mooring from a monohull or else a magical sunrise next to the Île d'Yeu from a catamaran: there are so many things to do and see when cruising, especially as you find yourself in the heart of nature.

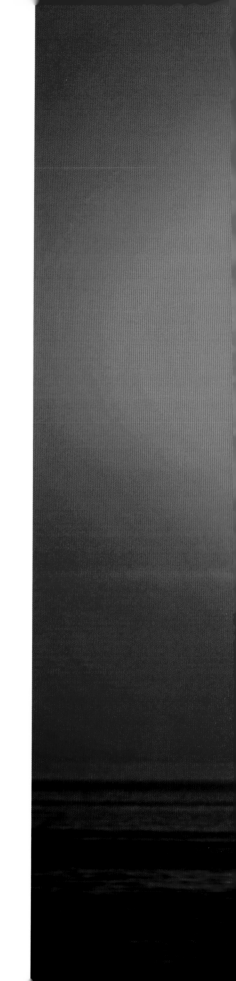

Southern latitudes

The light is different here. It's harsher, more prying, clearer. Something to do with a hole in the ozone layer or the absence of land around the latitudes of the Furious Fifties. One thing is certain: nature here is nothing like anywhere else. The strength of the wind, the height of the surrounding mountains, the steepness of the ice-covered cliffs plunging straight into the water, the size of the waves – or rather the mountains of sea that circulate around the ocean – the depth of the depressions that hit the Andes mountains, the ruggedness of the few people who live here, the density of vegetable life, the cold, the damp... Inhospitable Patagonia, land of fire. It's tricky to visit because there's so little protection from the changeable weather, but it's powerful and unforgettable.

Nature
Human beings are rare in Patagonia, as are animals. Those we meet, on land as well as in the water, seem to come from nowhere. And for good reasons: they are in the middle of nowhere.

The Horn
The famous Cape Horn on a bad day. A gust of wind is picking up, the waves become moving hills and water will soon be flying as it knocks against the williwaws.

Power
(previous double-page spread) All the atmosphere of the Patagonian canals during the 'high' season. Tall mountains, low skies, a heavy wind that comes down in bursts, dark and freezing waters, an improbable agglomeration placed there by accident. Not hostile, but nearly. Powerful, in any case.

Shenandoah
Approaching the Garibaldi glacier, the American three-masted *Shenandoah*, which now sails under the Italian flag, is part of a select group of large yachts brave enough to go around the world and to venture into Patagonia. A spectacle on a par with the prestige of these great circumnavigators.

Wally and friends

Esense
Without doubt one of the most beautiful boats on earth, the Wally *Esense*, which is 143ft (43.7m) long and has almost that much teak on her deck. Her unique mast can support 9,688sq ft (900m²) of sail, but the helmsman can sail her alone thanks to her hydraulic systems. Superlative sailing.

Welcome to the superior world of superyachts, where it's all about luxury, grace and gratifying the senses. Access is strictly reserved for those who can afford the most beautiful boats in the world.

The world of superyachts is in another universe altogether. It's a galaxy apart, where the dream would be the essence, luxe and quality, the raw material, aesthetism and the perfect details of the gravitation force. A world where concerns about length, power and weight are secondary. Oh, yes, and a place where money is the life-giving oxygen! But let's not talk about money – that only reveals we don't have enough.

With that as the starting point, there are many options. You can buy an existing yacht, which is easier than it sounds because most superyachts are put up for sale or for charter after just a few years' use. The brokers' lists confirm this: the quantity of boats available is only matched by the number of idyllic destinations where they can be found.

This buoyant bargain market is explained by the fact that a yacht owner starting from scratch will have to wait for several years before being able to play with their new toy. This doesn't sit well with a type of person who, by definition, is used to having everything right away. Building a new boat is a long journey with many stops along the way, not all of them very exciting. First you have to find a project manager, a naval architect, an interior designer, an office and a shipyard, then you have to work with them on the lines, the interior layout, the functionality, the operating systems, and the tenders, all the while negotiating with banks and insurance brokers, as well as changing your mind about everything several times – all of which will easily take up a whole year.

After all that, the actual boatbuilding gets started and often takes two or three years. If you are building the ultimate yacht, you'll have to hold your horses because, generally speaking, there will be delays. Then at last comes launch day, which is around the time the crew are hired,

followed by sea trials and final works before delivery, which will take another few months if all goes well. You have to be very determined, very patient and thoroughly protected from any financial crash or other change in fortune that might befall you along the way. Joking apart, this happens frequently, and there's nothing worse or more complicated than a project that is interrupted while in progress.

Exceptionality made to measure

Another option is to hand over your project to a shipyard with experience in this area. That's how the heavyweights at the top end of the yachting business operate, and it's how the Wally concept was born, with an interesting variation: its founder, Luca Bassani, went through all the trials of being an owner before changing sides and becoming a builder. He therefore knows what he's talking about and, above all, what his clients don't want to talk about.

Bassani is to the yachting industry what Enzo Ferrari was to cars. He's a visionary figure who, using ideas borrowed from the racing world, has managed to create a dynasty of boats that are unique not only in appearance but in performance. Traditionally, superyachts were usually heavy, pot-bellied boats that equated comfort with excess, both in terms of décor and weight.

Wally transformed the look of luxury sailing yachts by applying a minimalist aesthetic that cleared the decks of almost all visible fittings, and improved their performance by using hydraulic power and computerisation to simplify all aspects of sailing. Yachts longer than 100ft (30m) can nowadays be manoeuvred with just two fingers, which in turn reduces to the minimum the amount of crew needed to run

Indio
Indio's tiller post, another of the Wally shipyard's great successes. The two-way mirror houses the half-level rear saloon with sea views.

them. In any case, it's certainly better to have qualified electricians and mechanics on board than strong arms.

Dream maker

Aside from the product, the way the boats have been packaged has also started a trend. As well as using striking images for his sales literature – featuring one person at the helm, with no one else on deck – Bassani has organised regattas for Wally boats so that owners can enjoy, both on land and at sea, the standards to which they are accustomed.

Other superyachts owners have taken the more radical approach of converting large working boats such as ice breakers, ocean-going tugs and even racing catamarans, such as the former Club Med, winner of The Race in 2001, which is now fully fitted out – soberly, it must be said – and circles the world at speeds not recommended for cruising, from one cruising paradise to another!

From the photographic point of view, it's also exceptional. It's especially demanding because you are expected to deliver a standard of photography that matches the yacht and for clients who are used to perfection. But the time spent on a superyacht is always exhilarating. You always wonder how anyone could conceive, finance and build objects of such incredible shape, luxury and elegance simply for the pleasure of sailing. It's all amazing, delightful and ultimately fairly easy to photograph because it's already aesthetically pleasing and perfectly maintained. To have a superyacht and its crew at your disposal for three days to produce the best shots possible is both to have great trust placed in you and also great pressure! Sailing, anchorages, decks, interior shots, exterior shots, aerial views, tenders and toys – there is plenty of work

to be done. But to find yourself alone on the deck of a 130ft (40m) boat sailing silently, bathed in a beautiful light and a light breeze, with just a helmsman looking for the perfect sailing angle, and to have no other purpose than to make everything look even more beautiful, is not only an exceptional privilege but also a real happiness for anyone who loves sailing and yachts.

Maltese Falcon
In another very different vein, but just as exceptional, the *Maltese Falcon* experiments with a completely automated rigging system, which allows the rolling up of different sails to be controlled from the cockpit.

Design
(top and above) From the concealed fittings to the treatment of the light, from the choice of materials to the functionality of the space, from internal perspectives to the general aesthetics, quality design is ever-present on board modern superyachts. A fruitful field of investigation for architects and designers alike.

Teak decks
(left) The *Esense*'s deck has absolutely pure lines and is covered entirely with teak. Just a 'small' rounded deck saloon interrupts this purity of the lines. The deck fittings and technology are concealed within the lateral guard rail.

Gaffers
(right) The huge schooner *Adela* (180ft/55m) is equipped with a battened mizzen. This superyacht's sails are absolutely superb and she is frequently seen at superyacht get-togethers around the world.

W130

(below and bottom right) Huge sun deck, tapered hull and unparalleled performance for the silver grey Wally 130, designed by the Spaniard Javier Soto Acebal and launched in 2009.

Luca

(left) Luca Bassani on board the Wallynano, the smallest yacht he created.

Better Place

(left) A well-chosen name for one of the largest Wally yachts ever built, which has an upper deck nestled under an imposing deck saloon hidden behind opaque bay windows.

A life more beautiful

It's the magical hour that follows or precedes sunset, when everything is calm, and when superyachts compete with their sophisticated lighting. The pretty ladies in summer dresses will soon appear with a shawl wrapped around their shoulders to avoid the chill of the evening humidity. Porto Rotondo, Palma or Saint-Jean-Cap-Ferrat?

Athena
(previous double-page spread) Launched in 2004 by Royal Huisman, *Athena* is one of the biggest sailboats in the world and the biggest entirely built out of aluminium. She is 295ft (90m) long but her internal facilities only cater for … ten guests maximum!

Foredeck
The table is set for eight guests on the Wally 118's foredeck at Cala di Volpe, close to Porto Cervo. Exquisite.

Red night
Lighting effects from an interposed LED strip on board the Wally 130.

Good morning
(right) The sound of the motor running can't be heard, hardly a splutter from the cooling system either. Soon it will be time to cast off for another day of sailing between the Kornati Islands.

James Bond
(left and above) The Wally 118 has an incredible futuristic look that revolutionised the way people view motorised superyachts when it was released in 2005. With 17,000hp produced by three gas turbine engines, cruising speed can reach up to 60 knots …

Futuristic
(right) The design of medium-sized motor yachts changed enormously during the first decade of the noughties. Stretched and purified lines and large tinted bay windows to make the most of the landscape, this is a far cry from the motorboats of yore with starched lines.

(following double-page spreads)
Another world
The world of superyachts knows very few limits when it comes to size, sophistication or the way to manage projects and their execution. Another world.

Setting sun
End of the day at Les Voiles de Saint-Tropez, an unmissable event to see all that is beautiful and which sails.

Acknowledgements

This collection of images wouldn't have seen the light of day without the help of a number of contributors who I would like to thank from the bottom of my heart, most notably:

The owners, builders, crews and navigators without whom the sea would be without sails, sailing boats and the wonderful spectacle they provide all year round.

All the race and maritime festival organisers, clubs, associations and communities, along with their teams of volunteers, without whom nothing would get done, especially the Société Nautique de Marseille, Yachting Club de la Pointe Rouge, Cercle Nautique et Touristique du Lacydon, Yacht Club de France, Société Nautique de Saint-Tropez, Yacht club de Cannes, Yacht Club de Monaco and Golden Gate Yacht Club.

The press boats and helicopter pilots who enable us to travel through sea and sky to take our photos, especially Didier Vaultier, Laurence Desmasures, Thierry Leignac and Jacques Ripert.

My colleagues Guilain Grenier, Catherine Menicucci, Joanna Marut and Marie-Antoinette de Meo, who undertake daily to manage the unmanageable.

Our faithful clients in the maritime industry, Bénéteau, Fountaine-Pajot, Wally Yachts and Nautitech.

The competitors who trusted us and allowed us on board, including Yann Eliès, Kito de Pavant, Bruno Peyron, Loick Peyron, Michel Desjoyeaux, Jeremie Beyou, Thomas Coville, Alain Thébault, the team at France de Voile, James Spithill and the team at ORACLE Team USA, the skippers and crews of *Pen Duick*, *Altaïr*, *Tuiga*, *Mariquita*, *Atlantic* and *Shenandoah*.

My colleagues and partners in the community of nautical photographers Sea and Co, Philip Plisson, Guillaume Plisson, and Christian Février.

Special thanks to those who helped us follow the epic America's Cup from the inside, Mr Larry Ellison, Judith Sim, Chris Dickson, Russell Coutts, Stephen Barclay, Jane Eagleson, Tim Jeffery, Peter Rusch and the staff at the America's Cup Event Authority and the America's Cup Race Management.

Thanks also to the PR professionals who act as vital links between the photographers and the sportsmen and women, especially the Windreport agency, the Mille et une vagues agency, Maguelonne Turcat, Isabel Genis, Hélène de Fontainieu, Monica Paolazzi, Julia Huvé, Fabienne Morin, Vincent Borde, Corine Renié-Peretié, Stéphanie Nadin, Bernard Schöpfer, Bruno Troublé, Christine Bélanger and the PR team at Louis Vuitton.

A special nod to *Voiles et Voiliers* magazine and the team led by Pierre Lavialle, Didier Ravon and Hervé Hillard, with thanks for their loyalty. Not forgetting Daniel Allisy, even if he prefers to go sailing these days.

Finally, a permanent thank you to my wife and my sons who, when they weren't acting as my models or pilots, were always willing to pack their bags and follow me, and who always supported me unstintingly during the long absences that are part and parcel of this fantastic vocation I've dedicated myself to for the past 30 years.

Published by Adlard Coles Nautical
an imprint of Bloomsbury Publishing Plc
50 Bedford Square, London WC1B 3DP
www.adlardcoles.com

Bloomsbury is a trademark of Bloomsbury Publishing Plc

First published as *Gilles Martin-Raget: vu en mer* by
Editions du Chêne-Hachette Livre, 2014
Copyright © 2014 Editions du Chêne-Hachette, 2014

Copyright © Gilles Martin-Raget 2014
Photographs by Gilles Martin-Raget

First published by Adlard Coles Nautical in 2014

ISBN 978–1–4729–1165–0
ePDF 978–1–4729–1476–7
ePub 978–1–4729–1522–1

A CIP catalogue record for this book is available from the British Library.

This book is produced using paper that is made from wood grown in managed, sustainable forests. It is natural, renewable and recyclable. The logging and manufacturing processes conform to the environmental regulations of the country of origin.

Typeset in 11pt on 13.5pt Helvetic Neue LT Std
by Margaret Brain, Wisbech, Cambs

Printed by Midas Printing in China

Note: while all reasonable care has been taken in the publication of this book, the publisher takes no responsibility for the use of the methods or products described in the book.

10 9 8 7 6 5 4 3 2 1